Growing with Purpose: Strategies and Techniques for Scaling and Sustaining Business Expansion

From Survival to Thriving - A Mission Plan for Strategic Growth and Sustainable Success

Dr. Reginald D. Johnson Jr.

Learning and Development Manager, Innovator, Educator, Business Consultant with an I.T. Focus

COPYRIGHT AND DISCLAIMERS

do not make any representations or warranties, express or implied, regarding the completeness, accuracy, reliability, suitability, or availability of the content or any related graphics contained within. Any reliance you place on such information is strictly at your own discretion and risk. We disclaim any liability for loss or damage, whether direct or indirect, arising from the use of this material. It is advisable to seek professional advice or conduct further research specific to your business needs before making any significant decisions.

Trademark Disclaimer:

All product names, logos, and brands mentioned in this book are the property of their respective owners. Their inclusion in this book does not imply endorsement, sponsorship, or affiliation. The use of such names, logos, and brands does not imply that they are free from copyright or other proprietary rights. The use of these names, logos, and brands is purely for illustrative purposes and to provide examples within the context of the content.

Table of Contents

Message From the Author

Welcome to the third installment of "The Entrepreneur's Roadmap Series: Mastering the Fundamentals of Starting, Funding, and Growing Your Business." In this book, titled "Growing with Purpose: Strategies and Techniques for Scaling and Sustaining Business Expansion," we will delve into the crucial aspects of taking your business to the next level and ensuring its sustainable success.

Building upon the foundation established in the previous two books, "Starting Strong" and "Funding Your Vision," we now shift our focus to the exciting phase of growth and expansion. This book is designed to equip entrepreneurs and business owners, like yourself, with the knowledge, strategies, and techniques needed to assess growth opportunities, optimize operations, diversify markets, develop effective marketing strategies, foster innovation, cultivate leadership, and overcome growth challenges.

By following the guidance and lessons shared throughout this book, you will gain a comprehensive understanding of the intricacies involved in scaling and sustaining a business. Each chapter is carefully crafted to provide practical insights, real-life examples, and actionable tips that will engage and empower you as you embark on your growth journey.

Whether you are a startup founder seeking to accelerate growth, a small business owner looking to expand into new markets, or an established entrepreneur aiming to sustain your success, "Growing with Purpose" will serve as your mission plan for strategic growth and sustainable expansion.

Now, let's dive into the first chapter and explore the importance of assessing growth opportunities to identify potential areas for business expansion.

Part 1: Setting the Stage for Growth

Chapter 1: Assessing Growth Opportunities

⎯•◇•⎯

Introduction

In the journey of business growth and expansion, one of the fundamental pillars is the thorough assessment of growth opportunities. This chapter highlights the critical importance of assessing growth opportunities and provides practical guidance on the methods, frameworks, and strategies to identify potential areas for business expansion. By conducting proper assessment, businesses can position themselves for strategic growth and sustainable success.

Section 1: The Significance of Assessing Growth Opportunities

Assessing growth opportunities is a pivotal undertaking for any business aspiring to expand its horizons and achieve long-term success. It serves as the compass that guides strategic decision-making, helping businesses identify potential areas for expansion and align their efforts accordingly. By thoroughly assessing growth opportunities, businesses gain a deeper understanding of the market landscape, customer demands, and competitive dynamics, allowing them to position themselves strategically and increase their chances of thriving in a rapidly evolving business environment.

1. **Identifying Untapped Markets and Customer Segments**

Assessing growth opportunities enables businesses to identify untapped markets and customer segments ripe for exploration. By examining market data and trends, businesses can uncover gaps and unmet needs, offering them the chance to develop innovative solutions that resonate with potential customers. Through careful analysis of demographics, preferences, and emerging consumer behaviors, businesses can uncover new avenues for growth and tailor their products or services to capture these opportunities effectively.

2. **Staying Ahead of Competitors**

In a competitive business landscape, assessing growth opportunities allows businesses to stay ahead of their rivals. By thoroughly understanding the competitive landscape, including the strengths, weaknesses, and strategies of key competitors, businesses can differentiate themselves and develop unique value propositions. This knowledge empowers businesses to anticipate competitive threats, capitalize on white spaces, and identify areas where they can outperform their rivals, thus positioning themselves as leaders in their respective markets.

3. **Minimizing Risks through Aligned Strategies**

Assessing growth opportunities helps businesses minimize risks associated with expansion. By conducting meticulous research and analysis, businesses can assess the viability and potential returns of each growth opportunity. This evaluation process allows them to align their expansion strategies with market demand, mitigating the risks of entering saturated markets or pursuing ventures with limited growth potential. With a clear understanding of the risks involved, businesses can make informed decisions and allocate their resources effectively, increasing their chances of sustainable growth.

4. Capitalizing on Emerging Trends and Technologies

Market dynamics are constantly evolving, driven by emerging trends and technological advancements. Assessing growth opportunities equips businesses with the tools to capitalize on these shifts. By keeping a close eye on market trends, consumer preferences, and disruptive technologies, businesses can identify emerging opportunities that align with their strengths and capabilities. This proactive approach enables businesses to adapt their offerings, seize early-mover advantages, and establish themselves as industry leaders in the face of rapid change.

Assessing growth opportunities is an indispensable step in the journey of business expansion. By identifying untapped markets, staying ahead of competitors, minimizing risks through aligned strategies, and capitalizing on emerging trends, businesses can position themselves for success. In the following sections, we will delve deeper into the methods and frameworks for evaluating growth opportunities, providing practical guidance on conducting market research, and showcasing real-world examples of businesses that successfully identified and capitalized on growth opportunities. By immersing ourselves in these insights, we can empower ourselves to make informed decisions and embark on a path of strategic growth and sustainable success.

Section 2: Methods and Frameworks for Evaluating Growth Opportunities

When it comes to evaluating growth opportunities, businesses need to employ a systematic approach that considers various factors influencing their expansion potential. This section delves into different methods and frameworks for evaluating growth opportunities, providing businesses with the necessary tools to assess market potential, understand the competitive landscape, and gauge customer demand. By utilizing these methods and frameworks, businesses can make informed decisions that align with their growth objectives and increase their chances of success in the ever-changing business landscape.

1. **Market Potential Assessment**

   To evaluate growth opportunities effectively, businesses must assess the market potential of different segments and industries. This involves analyzing market size, growth rates, and trends to identify areas with the most favorable prospects. By understanding the size and growth potential of a market, businesses can determine if it offers the scale necessary for expansion and if it aligns with their long-term goals. Various analytical tools, such as market research reports, industry databases, and trend analysis, can provide valuable insights into market potential.

2. **Competitive Landscape Analysis**

   Understanding the competitive landscape is crucial in evaluating growth opportunities. Businesses must assess the strengths, weaknesses, strategies, and market positioning of their competitors. This analysis helps businesses identify gaps or weaknesses that can be exploited to gain a competitive advantage. By examining competitors' offerings, target markets, pricing strategies, and distribution channels, businesses can better understand their own positioning and determine how to differentiate themselves effectively. Tools such as competitive intelligence, industry reports, and market analysis can aid in conducting a comprehensive competitive landscape analysis.

3. Customer Demand Evaluation

Assessing customer demand is essential for identifying growth opportunities that resonate with target customers. Businesses must conduct in-depth research to understand customer preferences, needs, and evolving behaviors. This can involve surveys, focus groups, customer interviews, and data analysis to gather insights into what customers want and how their needs are changing. By understanding customer demand, businesses can tailor their products, services, and marketing strategies to meet the evolving expectations of their target audience.

4. SWOT Analysis

A SWOT analysis (Strengths, Weaknesses, Opportunities, and Threats) is a widely used framework that provides a holistic view of the internal and external factors influencing a business's growth potential. By evaluating internal strengths and weaknesses, businesses can identify areas where they have a competitive advantage and areas that require improvement. Examining external opportunities and threats allows businesses to identify potential growth avenues and anticipate potential challenges or risks. A SWOT analysis provides a structured framework for businesses to assess their current position and make strategic decisions based on their unique strengths and the opportunities available in the market.

By utilizing these evaluation methods and frameworks, businesses can gain a comprehensive understanding of growth opportunities and make informed decisions regarding their expansion plans. These tools provide a systematic approach to evaluating market potential, assessing the competitive landscape, understanding customer demand, and considering internal factors. Armed with this knowledge, businesses can prioritize growth opportunities that align with their capabilities and develop strategies to capitalize on them effectively.

In the next section, we will delve into practical guidance on conducting market research, analyzing industry trends, and identifying growth drivers. By combining these insights with the methods and frameworks discussed in this section, businesses can further refine their assessment of growth opportunities and set the stage for successful expansion.

Section 3: Practical Guidance on Conducting Market Research and Identifying Growth Drivers

To effectively assess growth opportunities, businesses need to conduct comprehensive market research and identify the key drivers that will propel their expansion. This section provides practical guidance on conducting market research, analyzing industry trends, and identifying growth drivers. By following these guidelines, businesses can gather valuable insights and make informed decisions that lay the foundation for successful growth.

1. **Conducting Market Research**

   Market research is a crucial component of assessing growth opportunities. It involves gathering and analyzing relevant data to gain insights into customer behavior, market dynamics, and industry trends. To conduct effective market research, businesses can follow these practical steps:

   a. *Define Research Objectives:* Clearly define the goals and objectives of the research. Determine what specific insights you aim to gather and how they will contribute to identifying growth opportunities.

b. ***Choose Research Methods:*** Select the most appropriate research methods based on your objectives and available resources. This may include surveys, interviews, focus groups, observation, or data analysis.

c. ***Collect Primary and Secondary Data:*** Gather both primary and secondary data to ensure a comprehensive understanding of the market. Primary data is collected directly from customers or target audiences, while secondary data refers to existing information from external sources such as market reports, industry publications, and government databases.

d. ***Analyze and Interpret Data:*** Analyze the collected data to uncover patterns, trends, and insights. Interpret the findings to identify growth opportunities and key areas for business expansion.

2. **Analyzing Industry Trends**

   Evaluating industry trends is essential for identifying growth opportunities and staying ahead of the competition. By analyzing trends, businesses can anticipate market shifts, emerging customer needs, and technological advancements. Here's practical guidance for analyzing industry trends:

   a. ***Monitor Industry Publications:*** Stay updated on industry-specific publications, reports, and journals to understand the latest trends, innovations, and market developments.

   b. ***Attend Conferences and Trade Shows:*** Participate in conferences and trade shows related to your industry. These events provide opportunities to learn about emerging trends, network with industry experts, and gain valuable insights.

c. ***Engage with Industry Thought Leaders:*** Follow thought leaders and experts in your industry through blogs, social media, and professional networks. Engage in discussions and stay connected to gain insights into industry trends and best practices.

d. ***Leverage Online Resources:*** Utilize online resources such as market research reports, industry blogs, and trend analysis tools to gain a comprehensive understanding of industry trends and their implications.

3. **Identifying Growth Drivers**

   Identifying growth drivers is crucial for assessing the potential of each opportunity and making informed decisions. These drivers act as catalysts for business expansion and can vary based on the industry, market dynamics, and customer demands. Here are practical steps to identify growth drivers:

   a. ***Analyze Customer Needs:*** Understand the evolving needs and preferences of your target customers. Identify the specific pain points or desires that your products or services can address.

   b. ***Assess Market Dynamics:*** Evaluate the market dynamics, including factors such as demand-supply balance, competitive landscape, regulatory environment, and technological advancements. Identify how these factors can contribute to or hinder your growth prospects.

   c. ***Identify Emerging Opportunities:*** Look for emerging opportunities resulting from changes in consumer behavior, advancements in technology, or market gaps. These opportunities may present new markets, customer segments, or product/service innovations that can drive growth.

d. **Consider Competitive Advantages:** Assess your competitive advantages and unique value proposition. Determine how these strengths can position you for growth and differentiate you from competitors.

By following these practical guidelines, businesses can conduct effective market research, analyze industry trends, and identify the key growth drivers that will propel their expansion efforts. Armed with this valuable information, businesses can make informed decisions and strategically pursue growth opportunities that align with their capabilities and long-term objectives.

In the next section, we will share real-world examples and case studies of businesses that successfully identified and capitalized on growth opportunities. These practical illustrations will provide further insights and inspiration, demonstrating how businesses can turn their assessment of growth opportunities into tangible success stories.

Section 4: Real-World Examples and Case Studies

Real-world examples and case studies offer invaluable insights into how businesses have successfully identified and capitalized on growth opportunities. By examining these examples, you can gain a deeper understanding of the practical application of assessing growth opportunities and the strategies employed by successful businesses. These stories provide inspiration and actionable lessons that can guide you in your own pursuit of growth.

1   Identifying Market Gaps and Innovative Solutions

Numerous successful businesses have identified market gaps and developed innovative solutions to meet customer needs. For example, consider the rise of ride-sharing companies like Uber and Lyft. They recognized the untapped potential of the transportation market and leveraged technology to disrupt the traditional taxi industry. By assessing the demand for convenient, on-demand transportation services and addressing the pain points of customers, these companies seized the opportunity to revolutionize an industry.

Similarly, companies like Airbnb recognized the gap in the hospitality sector and tapped into the sharing economy. By providing an online platform for individuals to rent out their spare rooms or properties, they created a new market segment and disrupted the traditional hotel industry. These examples showcase how businesses that assess market gaps and offer innovative solutions can achieve remarkable growth and success.

2   Expanding into New Geographical Markets

Expanding into new geographical markets can be a powerful growth strategy for businesses. One notable example Is the international expansion of tech giant Amazon. By assessing the potential of global e-commerce, Amazon strategically entered new markets, establishing its presence in various countries. Through extensive market research, they identified the demand for online retail and tailored their services to suit the unique needs and preferences of each market. By assessing growth opportunities in different regions, Amazon experienced exponential growth and became a global leader in e-commerce.

3   Targeting Niche Customer Segments

Targeting niche customer segments can be a lucrative growth strategy for businesses. For instance, consider the success of Lululemon, a renowned athletic apparel brand. Rather than targeting a broad market, Lululemon assessed the growth opportunities within the yoga and fitness segment. By understanding the unique needs and preferences of this niche customer group, Lululemon developed high-quality, stylish activewear tailored to their specific requirements. This focused approach allowed them to capture a loyal customer base and achieve significant growth within their targeted niche.

4   Adapting Products or Services to Emerging Trends

Successful businesses often assess emerging trends and adapt their products or services accordingly. A prime example is Apple's transformation from a computer company to a leader in consumer electronics. Recognizing the rising demand for portable music players, Apple introduced the iPod, revolutionizing the music industry. They continued to assess market trends and adapted their product lineup, introducing the iPhone, iPad, and other innovative devices that shaped the way we interact with technology. By assessing growth opportunities stemming from emerging trends, Apple has maintained its position as a global powerhouse.

These real-world examples demonstrate the transformative power of assessing growth opportunities. By recognizing market gaps, expanding into new geographical markets, targeting niche customer segments, and adapting to emerging trends, businesses can achieve substantial growth and carve out a competitive advantage.

Conclusion

In conclusion, assessing growth opportunities is a crucial step in the journey of scaling and sustaining business expansion. By evaluating market potential, competitive landscape, and customer demand, you can identify areas for business growth and development. Through conducting market research, analyzing industry trends, and identifying growth drivers, you can make informed decisions and prioritize strategic initiatives. Real-world examples and case studies have demonstrated how businesses successfully identified and capitalized on growth opportunities, inspiring you to apply these principles to your own ventures. Remember, by proactively assessing growth opportunities, you can position your business for sustainable success and thrive in a dynamic marketplace. In the subsequent chapters, we will delve deeper into various growth strategies, techniques, and best practices.

Chapter 2: Scaling Your Operations and Infrastructure

Introduction

Scaling operations and infrastructure is a critical step in supporting business growth and ensuring its long-term success. In this chapter, we will highlight the significance of scaling and provide practical strategies to optimize processes, improve efficiency, and manage resources effectively. We will explore techniques for expanding production capacity, enhancing supply chain management, leveraging technology, and building a high-performing team. Real-life examples and case studies will illustrate how businesses have successfully scaled their operations, providing valuable insights and actionable tips for your own growth journey.

Section 1: Significance of Scaling Operations and Infrastructure

Scaling operations and infrastructure is a critical undertaking for businesses aiming to support their growth objectives and achieve long-term success. As your business expands, the demands placed on your operational capabilities increase significantly. It becomes essential to scale your operations and infrastructure to meet growing customer demand, improve efficiency and productivity, and manage resources effectively. This section will delve into the significance of scaling and highlight the key reasons why it is crucial for your business's sustained growth.

1. **Meeting Growing Demand**

   One of the primary reasons to scale your operations and infrastructure is to meet the rising customer demand that accompanies business growth. As your customer base expands or your existing customers demand more of your products or services, it becomes imperative to have the necessary capacity and resources in place to fulfill their needs. By scaling your operations, you can ensure that you have the ability to deliver products or services promptly, maintain consistent quality, and meet customer expectations. Failure to scale effectively may result in missed opportunities, dissatisfied customers, and damage to your brand reputation.

2. **Improving Efficiency and Productivity**

   Scaling operations provides an opportunity to optimize processes, improve efficiency, and enhance productivity within your organization. As your business grows, it is important to critically evaluate your existing processes and identify areas for improvement. By streamlining workflows, eliminating bottlenecks, and implementing automation or technology solutions, you can enhance operational efficiency. This, in turn, allows you to handle larger volumes of work without incurring significant additional costs or sacrificing quality. Improved efficiency and productivity not only enable you to meet growing demand effectively but also contribute to cost savings, higher profitability, and increased competitiveness.

3. **Managing Resources Effectively**

Efficient resource management is another crucial aspect of scaling operations and infrastructure. As your business grows, it becomes imperative to allocate resources effectively and strategically. This includes managing financial resources, inventory, equipment, and personnel efficiently to support your growth objectives. Scaling operations allows you to optimize resource allocation and utilization, ensuring that resources are directed towards areas that drive growth and generate the highest return on investment. Effective resource management also helps you minimize waste, reduce costs, and maintain a healthy financial position as your business expands.

By scaling your operations and infrastructure, you can position your business for sustained growth, adapt to increasing customer demand, and optimize resource allocation. This not only enables you to meet customer expectations efficiently but also provides a solid foundation for further expansion and success. Realizing the significance of scaling your operations and infrastructure is the first step towards building a strong growth-oriented business.

In the subsequent sections, we will explore strategies for optimizing processes, improving efficiency, managing resources effectively, expanding production capacity, enhancing supply chain management, leveraging technology, and building a high-performing team. Additionally, we will provide real-life examples and case studies of businesses that effectively scaled their operations, showcasing how these strategies can be applied in practice to achieve tangible growth outcomes.

Section 2: Strategies for Optimizing Processes, Improving Efficiency, and Managing Resources Effectively

Scaling operations and infrastructure requires implementing strategies that optimize processes, improve efficiency, and enable effective resource management. These strategies are essential for ensuring smooth operations, maximizing productivity, and supporting business growth. In this section, we will explore various techniques and best practices to help you streamline operations, reduce waste, and manage resources efficiently.

1. **Process Streamlining**

   Process streamlining involves evaluating and improving existing workflows to eliminate inefficiencies and enhance productivity. By streamlining processes, you can reduce unnecessary steps, minimize delays, and improve overall operational efficiency. Here are key steps to consider:

   a. ***Process Evaluation:*** Conduct a comprehensive review of your current processes to identify bottlenecks, redundancies, or areas that require improvement. Engage with employees at different levels to gain insights into their experiences and challenges within the existing workflows.

   b. ***Identify Opportunities for Automation:*** Explore automation tools and technologies that can streamline repetitive tasks, reduce human errors, and free up valuable time and resources. Automation can range from implementing software solutions for data entry and reporting to integrating robotic process automation (RPA) for more complex tasks.

c. ***Standardize Workflows:*** Establish clear standard operating procedures (SOPs) that outline best practices and guidelines for each process. This helps ensure consistency, reduces confusion, and enables efficient training for new employees.

d. ***Continuous Improvement:*** Encourage a culture of continuous improvement within your organization. Regularly seek feedback from employees and stakeholders, and use their input to refine processes and identify opportunities for further optimization.

2. **Lean Methodologies**

Applying lean methodologies helps eliminate waste, reduce costs, and optimize resource allocation. Here are some key strategies to consider:

a. ***Just-in-Time (JIT) Inventory Management:*** Adopt JIT principles to minimize inventory carrying costs and reduce waste. With JIT, you maintain lean inventory levels by ordering or producing items only when they are needed, thus avoiding overstocking or stockouts.

b. ***Value Stream Mapping:*** Map out your value streams to identify areas of waste or non-value-added activities. By visualizing the flow of materials, information, and activities, you can identify opportunities for improvement and optimize processes accordingly.

c. ***Continuous Improvement Initiatives:*** Implement frameworks such as Kaizen or Six Sigma to empower employees to contribute to process improvement. Encourage them to identify inefficiencies, suggest innovative solutions, and participate in problem-solving initiatives.

d. ***Waste Reduction Strategies:*** Employ waste reduction strategies such as 5S (Sort, Set in Order, Shine, Standardize, Sustain) to eliminate waste, improve organization, and enhance workplace efficiency.

3. **Performance Metrics and Key Performance Indicators (KPIs)**

   Implementing performance metrics and KPIs is crucial for monitoring and measuring operational efficiency. By tracking relevant metrics, you can identify areas requiring improvement and make data-driven decisions. Here are some considerations:

   a. ***Identify Relevant Metrics:*** Determine the key metrics that align with your business objectives and provide insights into operational performance. Examples may include cycle time, productivity, quality indicators, customer satisfaction, and resource utilization.

   b. ***Establish Baselines and Targets:*** Set benchmarks and targets for each metric to gauge progress and measure success. These targets should be realistic, specific, and aligned with your growth objectives.

   c. ***Implement Reporting and Analysis Systems:*** Develop robust reporting systems and data analysis capabilities to gather, analyze, and interpret performance data. This will enable you to identify trends, track performance against targets, and make informed decisions for process improvement.

By implementing these strategies for optimizing processes, improving efficiency, and managing resources effectively, you can establish a strong operational foundation to support your business's growth. In the subsequent sections, we will explore techniques for expanding production capacity, enhancing supply chain management, leveraging technology, and building a high-performing team. Real-life examples and case studies will illustrate how businesses effectively scaled their operations, providing valuable insights and actionable tips for your own growth journey.

Section 3: Techniques for Expanding Production Capacity, Enhancing Supply Chain Management, and Leveraging Technology

Expanding production capacity and effectively managing the supply chain are crucial components of scaling operations and infrastructure. As your business grows, it becomes necessary to meet increased customer demand and ensure a seamless flow of goods or services. This section explores techniques and best practices to expand production capacity, optimize supply chain management, and leverage technology to support your business's growth objectives.

1. **Expanding Production Capacity**

   Expanding production capacity involves increasing your ability to produce goods or deliver services to meet growing customer demand. Here are key techniques to consider:

   a. *Assess Current Production Processes:* Evaluate your existing production processes, identify inefficiencies, and determine areas for improvement. Understand the constraints that limit your production capacity and explore opportunities for optimization.

   b. *Identify Bottlenecks:* Identify bottlenecks or constraints within your production processes that limit output or efficiency. By addressing these bottlenecks, such as optimizing equipment utilization, improving workflow layouts, or investing in new technologies, you can increase production capacity.

c. **Invest in Technology and Automation:** Explore technologies and automation solutions that can enhance production efficiency and output. Automation can range from robotics and machine learning to advanced manufacturing technologies. By leveraging technology, you can streamline processes, reduce human error, and achieve higher production volumes.

d. **Implement Lean Manufacturing Principles:** Embrace lean manufacturing principles, such as reducing waste, improving cycle times, and optimizing inventory levels. Lean methodologies, such as Just-in-Time (JIT) production or Kanban systems, can help you eliminate non-value-added activities, minimize lead times, and improve overall production efficiency.

2. **Enhancing Supply Chain Management**

Effective supply chain management is vital for scaling operations and ensuring a seamless flow of materials, information, and services. Consider the following techniques:

a. **Supplier Relationship Management:** Foster strong relationships with suppliers by developing mutually beneficial partnerships, maintaining open lines of communication, and collaborating on improving supply chain performance. Establishing long-term relationships can result in better pricing, improved reliability, and faster response times.

b. **Demand Planning and Forecasting:** Implement robust demand planning and forecasting processes to accurately predict customer demand. By understanding demand patterns and trends, you can optimize inventory levels, prevent stockouts or overstocking, and align production with customer requirements.

c. **Streamline Logistics and Distribution:** Optimize your logistics and distribution networks to minimize lead times, reduce transportation costs, and enhance overall supply chain efficiency. Consider outsourcing certain logistics functions, implementing technology solutions for real-time tracking, or exploring alternative transportation modes to streamline operations.

d. **Risk Management and Resilience:** Mitigate supply chain risks by diversifying your supplier base, developing contingency plans, and staying updated on market conditions. Enhancing supply chain resilience helps your business navigate disruptions effectively and ensures business continuity during unexpected events.

3. **Leveraging Technology for Scalability**

Technology plays a crucial role in scaling operations and infrastructure. Consider the following techniques to leverage technology for scalability:

a. **Enterprise Resource Planning (ERP) Systems**: Implement ERP systems to integrate various business functions, streamline processes, and improve communication across different departments. ERP systems provide real-time visibility into operations, enabling better decision-making and resource allocation.

Imagine a retail business that implements an ERP system. This system integrates different aspects of the business, like sales, inventory, and finance, into a single platform. With the ERP system, the business can easily track inventory levels, monitor sales performance, and manage finances in real-time. This allows the business owner to make informed decisions about restocking inventory, identifying popular products, and allocating resources effectively.

b. ***Data Analytics and Business Intelligence***: Leverage data analytics and business intelligence tools to gain insights into operational performance, identify areas for improvement, and make data-driven decisions. Analyzing key performance indicators (KPIs) and using predictive analytics can help you optimize operations and anticipate future demand.

Think of a restaurant that uses data analytics and business intelligence tools. By analyzing customer data, such as ordering patterns and customer feedback, the restaurant can gain insights into its operational performance. This information helps them understand which menu items are popular, identify areas for improvement in service, and make data-driven decisions to enhance the overall dining experience.

c. ***Cloud Computing and Software-as-a-Service (SaaS):*** Embrace cloud computing and SaaS solutions to scale your IT infrastructure quickly, reduce upfront costs, and gain access to advanced technologies without significant investments. Cloud-based solutions offer scalability, flexibility, and enhanced collaboration.

Consider a small business owner who wants to manage customer relationships efficiently. Instead of investing in expensive servers and software, they choose to use a cloud-based Customer Relationship Management (CRM) system. This means the CRM software is hosted on the internet, allowing the business owner and their team to access it from anywhere using a web browser. They can easily track customer interactions, manage sales leads, and collaborate on customer-related tasks without worrying about the technical aspects of maintaining server infrastructure.

d. **Internet of Things (IoT) and Advanced Analytics:** Explore IoT devices and advanced analytics to collect real-time data from machines, processes, or products. This data can be used to optimize operations, improve maintenance schedules, and identify areas for efficiency gains.

    Picture a homeowner who installs smart devices in their house, such as a smart thermostat and smart lighting system. These IoT devices collect data on energy usage and patterns in the home. By using advanced analytics tools, the homeowner can analyze this data to identify energy-saving opportunities. For example, they can discover which appliances or habits consume the most energy and adjust save on their utility bills. Additionally, the IoT devices can be programmed to automatically adjust the temperature or turn off lights when the homeowner is not at home, providing convenience and energy efficiency.

By employing these techniques to expand production capacity, enhance supply chain management, and leverage technology, you can effectively scale your operations and support business growth. Real-life examples and case studies will further illustrate how businesses successfully implemented these strategies to achieve scalable operations. In the subsequent sections, we will provide actionable tips on hiring, training, and developing a high-performing team to support your business expansion.

Section 4: Actionable Tips on Hiring, Training, and Developing a High-Performing Team to Support Business Expansion

Building a high-performing team is essential for scaling operations and infrastructure effectively. As your business grows, you need a talented and motivated workforce that can adapt to evolving needs, drive innovation, and maintain operational excellence. This section explores actionable tips for hiring the right talent, training and developing your team, and fostering a culture of high performance.

1. **Hiring the Right Talent**

    a. *Clearly Define Job Roles and Requirements:* Before initiating the hiring process, clearly define the roles and responsibilities required to support your business's growth objectives. Outline the necessary skills, qualifications, and experience needed for each role. This clarity will enable you to attract candidates who are the best fit for your organization.

    b. *Develop Effective Recruitment Strategies*: Implement targeted recruitment strategies to attract top talent. Utilize various channels such as online job portals, professional networks, industry-specific platforms, and referrals. Craft compelling job descriptions and employer branding materials that communicate your organization's values, culture, and growth opportunities.

    c. *Conduct Thorough Interviews and Assessments:* Structure interviews to assess candidates' qualifications, skills, and cultural fit. Incorporate behavioral questions to understand their problem-solving abilities, adaptability, and collaboration skills. Consider implementing skill assessments, work simulations, or case studies to gauge candidates' capabilities.

d. *Cultural Fit Assessment:* Evaluate candidates' alignment with your organizational culture and values during the interview process. Assess their ability to thrive in a fast-paced and growth-oriented environment. Consider involving team members in the hiring process to gather multiple perspectives and ensure cultural fit.

2. **Training and Development**

   a. *Implement Onboarding Programs:* Develop comprehensive onboarding programs to facilitate the seamless integration of new hires into your organization. Provide them with the necessary tools, resources, and training to understand their roles, the company's mission, and the processes in place. Assign mentors or buddies to support their transition and foster a sense of belonging.

   b. *Continuous Learning Opportunities*: Encourage continuous learning and professional development by providing opportunities for training, workshops, seminars, and conferences. Support employees in acquiring new skills, staying updated with industry trends, and expanding their knowledge base. Emphasize the importance of a growth mindset and foster a culture of continuous improvement.

   c. *Cross-Functional Training:* Foster cross-functional collaboration and skill-sharing by providing opportunities for employees to work on projects outside their immediate roles. This enables them to gain a broader perspective, develop new skills, and contribute to the organization's growth objectives.

d. ***Performance Feedback and Coaching:*** Establish a culture of regular performance feedback and coaching. Provide constructive feedback to employees, recognize their achievements, and guide them in areas for improvement. Implement regular performance reviews to align individual goals with organizational objectives and identify development opportunities.

3. **Fostering a High-Performing Culture**

   a. ***Communication and Transparency:*** Foster open and transparent communication within your organization. Establish clear channels for information sharing, encourage feedback, and promote an inclusive environment where everyone's input is valued. Regularly communicate the company's goals, progress, and milestones to keep the team aligned and motivated.

   b. ***Empowerment and Autonomy:*** Delegate responsibilities and empower employees to make decisions within their areas of expertise. Encourage autonomy and ownership, allowing individuals to take initiative, explore innovative solutions, and contribute to the organization's growth objectives. Recognize and reward employees for their contributions.

   c. ***Collaboration and Teamwork:*** Promote a collaborative work environment where cross-functional teams can collaborate effectively. Encourage knowledge sharing, interdisciplinary cooperation, and a sense of collective accountability. Foster a culture that values diversity, inclusivity, and respect for differing perspectives.

   d. ***Employee Well-being and Work-Life Balance:*** Prioritize employee well-being and work-life balance. Create policies and practices that support a healthy work environment, provide flexibility where feasible, and promote the well-being of your team members. Encourage work-life integration and the importance of maintaining a sustainable work pace.

By implementing these actionable tips for hiring the right talent, training and developing your team, and fostering a high-performing culture, you can build a workforce capable of supporting your business expansion. Real-life examples and case studies will further illustrate how organizations effectively scaled their operations by investing in their human capital. In the subsequent section, we will provide insights on real-life businesses that successfully scaled their operations, showcasing their strategies and achievements. We will dive further into leadership and team development in Chapter 8.

Section 5: Real-Life Examples and Case Studies of Businesses that Effectively Scaled Their Operations

Real-life examples and case studies provide valuable insights into how well-known companies successfully scaled their operations and infrastructure. These stories offer practical knowledge and inspiration, showcasing strategies and approaches that have yielded significant growth and success. In this section, we will explore a range of businesses across various industries that effectively scaled their operations, providing you with concrete examples and lessons that you can apply to your own growth journey.

Case Study 1: Airbnb - Disrupting the Hospitality Industry

- Airbnb, a home-sharing platform, transformed the hospitality industry through its innovative approach to scaling operations. Starting as a small peer-to-peer rental platform, Airbnb effectively expanded its operations by leveraging the power of the sharing economy. By connecting homeowners with travelers seeking unique accommodation experiences, Airbnb quickly scaled its marketplace. Their success can be attributed to their ability to optimize processes and adapt to changing customer demands. Through strategic partnerships, including integration with travel booking platforms and property management software, Airbnb enhanced its reach and streamlined its operations. By focusing on user experience, customer trust, and building a strong community, Airbnb became a global leader in the hospitality industry, challenging traditional hotel chains.

Key Takeaway: By leveraging technology, strategic partnerships, and a customer-centric approach, businesses can disrupt established industries and achieve rapid growth.

Case Study 2: Warby Parker - Revolutionizing Eyewear Retail

- Warby Parker, an eyewear retailer, disrupted the traditional retail industry by offering affordable and stylish glasses directly to consumers. With a focus on cutting out middlemen and leveraging technology, Warby Parker scaled its operations efficiently. They employed a direct-to-consumer model, eliminating the need for brick-and-mortar stores and reducing costs. By embracing e-commerce and implementing a seamless online shopping experience, they attracted a large customer base. Warby Parker also prioritized customer service by offering virtual try-on options and free home try-on kits. Their commitment to social impact, such as donating glasses to those in need, resonated with customers, further fueling their growth. Through their innovative approach, Warby Parker disrupted the eyewear industry, gained market share, and expanded their product offerings.

Key Takeaway: Embracing e-commerce, direct-to-consumer models, and prioritizing customer experience can enable businesses to revolutionize traditional industries and achieve scalable growth.

Case Study 3: Slack - Transforming Communication and Collaboration

- Slack, a communication and collaboration platform, revolutionized the way teams work together. By offering a user-friendly interface and robust features, Slack gained popularity among businesses of all sizes. Their success can be attributed to their focus on enhancing productivity and streamlining communication. Slack effectively scaled its operations by integrating with other popular workplace tools, creating a seamless ecosystem for users. Through strategic partnerships and integrations, Slack extended its reach, allowing teams to communicate and collaborate more efficiently. Their commitment to continuous improvement and user feedback helped them stay ahead of the competition and maintain their position as a leader in the market.

Key Takeaway: By providing innovative solutions, integrating with complementary tools, and prioritizing user feedback, businesses can transform the way teams collaborate and achieve significant scalability.

These real-life examples illustrate how well-known companies effectively scaled their operations, disrupted industries, and achieved remarkable growth. By studying their strategies, innovations, and customer-centric approaches, you can gain valuable insights and apply relevant lessons to your own growth journey. In the subsequent chapters, we will continue to explore additional real-life examples and case studies that provide inspiration and practical guidance for scaling your business effectively.

Conclusion

In this chapter, we explored the significance of scaling operations and infrastructure to support business growth. We discussed strategies for optimizing processes, improving efficiency, and managing resources effectively. Additionally, we explored techniques for expanding production capacity, enhancing supply chain management, and leveraging technology. Lastly, we provided actionable tips on hiring, training, and developing a high-performing team to support business expansion.

By implementing these strategies and techniques, businesses can create a solid foundation for scaling their operations. Streamlining processes, embracing lean methodologies, and leveraging technology can result in improved productivity, reduced costs, and enhanced customer satisfaction. By expanding production capacity and optimizing supply chain management, businesses can meet growing customer demand and ensure a seamless flow of goods or services. Furthermore, hiring the right talent, providing comprehensive training, and fostering a high-performing culture are vital for building a team that can adapt to growth and drive success.

Throughout this chapter, we highlighted real-life examples and case studies of businesses that effectively scaled their operations. These examples serve as inspiration and provide practical insights into the strategies that led to their success. By learning from their experiences, you can apply relevant lessons to your own business and navigate the challenges of scaling with confidence.

As you continue reading, you will gain further insights into market expansion, effective marketing strategies, strategic partnerships, innovation, financial management, leadership development, overcoming growth challenges, and creating a comprehensive blueprint for success. Each chapter will provide you with valuable knowledge and real-world examples to guide you on your path to scaling and sustaining business expansion.

Remember, scaling operations and infrastructure requires careful planning, adaptability, and a focus on continuous improvement. By incorporating the strategies and techniques discussed in this chapter and throughout the book, you will be better equipped to scale your business and achieve sustainable growth.

Continue reading to discover the next chapters, where we will delve deeper into various aspects of scaling your business and provide you with the tools and knowledge necessary to thrive in the dynamic landscape of business expansion.

Part 2: Expanding Your Market Reach

Chapter 3: Market Expansion and Diversification

···◇◦·

Introduction

Section 1: Explaining the Concept of Market Expansion and Diversification as Strategies for Business Growth

In this section, we will explore two important strategies that businesses can use to achieve growth and tap into new opportunities: market expansion and diversification. Whether you're a budding entrepreneur or a business owner looking to take your company to the next level, understanding these concepts is essential for driving sustainable business success. Let's dive in and explore each strategy in more detail.

1. **Understanding Market Expansion**

    Market expansion refers to the process of entering new markets beyond your current customer base or geographic reach. It involves identifying untapped opportunities and strategically positioning your products or services to cater to the needs and preferences of these new markets. By expanding into new markets, you can open fresh avenues for growth and revenue generation.

    To effectively expand into new markets, it's crucial to conduct thorough market research. This involves understanding the target market's demographics, preferences, and purchasing behaviors. By gaining insights into the needs and desires of your prospective customers, you can tailor your products, marketing messages, and pricing strategies to resonate with them. Additionally, evaluating the competitive landscape and identifying unique selling points can help you differentiate your offerings and gain a competitive edge.

When considering market expansion, you have two primary approaches to choose from:

a. **Geographical Expansion**: This involves entering new regions, cities, or countries. It allows you to tap into new customer segments and leverage your existing strengths and expertise to establish a presence in new markets.

b. **Targeting New Customer Segments:** This approach involves identifying customer groups or niches that you haven't previously served. By understanding their specific needs and preferences, you can tailor your offerings to cater to these new customer segments effectively.

2. Exploring Diversification as a Growth Strategy

Diversification is the strategy of expanding the range of products or services your business offers. It allows you to tap into new markets, cater to evolving customer demands, and capitalize on new opportunities. By diversifying, you can reduce reliance on a single product or market, thereby minimizing risks and ensuring long-term sustainability.

Diversification can take various forms:

a. **Horizontal Diversification:** This involves offering new products or services that are related or complementary to your existing offerings. For example, a fitness equipment manufacturer may diversify into fitness apparel to cater to the broader needs of their customer base.

b. **Vertical Diversification:** This strategy entails expanding into different stages of the value chain. For instance, a coffee shop might diversify into coffee bean roasting or wholesale distribution.

c. **Conglomerate Diversification**: This involves entering entirely new industries or markets unrelated to your current business. For example, a technology company diversifying into the healthcare sector.

To successfully implement a diversification strategy, it's crucial to conduct a thorough analysis of market trends, customer needs, and the competitive landscape. This will help you identify gaps in the market and determine the best opportunities for expansion. Additionally, considering your core competencies, resources, and brand equity will ensure that your diversification efforts align with your overall business strategy.

3. **The Strategic Importance of Market Expansion and Diversification**

Both market expansion and diversification strategies are vital for driving business growth and maintaining a competitive edge. They offer several strategic benefits:

a. **Increased Market Share**: By expanding into new markets or diversifying your offerings, you can attract new customers and capture additional market share. This allows you to grow your customer base and generate more revenue.

b. **Risk Mitigation:** Relying on a single market or product can leave your business vulnerable to market fluctuations or changing customer preferences. Market expansion and diversification enable you to spread risks and reduce dependence on a single revenue source.

c. **Adaptability to Market Changes**: Markets are dynamic and ever-evolving. By embracing market expansion and diversification, your business becomes more adaptable to changes in customer behavior, technological advancements, and economic shifts. This flexibility ensures your long-term sustainability.

To effectively implement market expansion and diversification strategies, it's essential to conduct comprehensive market analysis, develop sound entry strategies, and adapt to local market dynamics. In the subsequent sections of this chapter, we will provide you with practical guidance on conducting market analysis, developing market entry strategies, and adapting your business to new market environments. Additionally, we will share real-life examples and case studies of businesses that have successfully expanded their markets or diversified their offerings. These examples will provide you with inspiration and actionable insights that you can apply to your own business growth journey.

Section 2: Approaches to Entering New Markets

In this section, we will explore different approaches to entering new markets as part of your business growth strategy. Whether you're considering expanding geographically or targeting new customer segments, choosing the right approach is essential for success. Let's delve into the various approaches and discover how they can help you unlock new growth opportunities.

1. **Geographical Expansion**

   Geographical expansion involves entering new regions, cities, or countries to reach a wider customer base and tap into new market potential. Here are key factors to consider when pursuing geographical expansion:

   a. **Thorough Market Research:** Conduct comprehensive market research to understand the target market's demographics, consumer preferences, cultural nuances, legal and regulatory requirements, and competitive landscape.

   b. **Tailored Offerings:** Adapt your products, services, and marketing strategies to resonate with the local audience effectively.

   c. **Replicating Success:** Leverage your existing brand reputation, products, or services that have proven successful in your current market.

   Geographical expansion offers several advantages, including:

   - *Market Potential:* Tap into untapped market potential in new regions or countries.

- *Diversification:* Reduce dependency on a single market and diversify your revenue streams.

- *Risk Mitigation:* Mitigate risks associated with economic fluctuations or market saturation in your existing market.

However, it's essential to carefully evaluate the costs, logistics, and scalability of expanding geographically to ensure a smooth transition and sustainable growth.

2. **Targeting New Customer Segments**

Targeting new customer segments involves identifying groups of customers who have distinct needs, preferences, or demographics that differ from your current customer base. Here's what you should consider when targeting new customer segments:

   a. **Thorough Market Research:** Conduct in-depth research to analyze the specific needs, pain points, buying behaviors, and preferred communication channels of the new customer segments.

   b. **Tailored Marketing Messages**: Craft targeted marketing messages that resonate with the unique characteristics of these customer segments.

   c. **Tailored Offerings:** Develop products or services that address the specific requirements of these new customer segments.

Targeting new customer segments offers several advantages, including:

   1. *Market Expansion*: Tap into previously unexplored markets and unlock new revenue streams.

2. *Competitive Edge:* Gain a competitive edge by catering to the unique needs of specific customer segments.

3. *Risk Mitigation*: Diversify your customer base to mitigate risks associated with over-reliance on a single segment.

However, it's crucial to carefully evaluate the market potential, competition, and feasibility of serving these new customer segments to ensure long-term success.

3. Evaluating the Right Approach for Your Business

When considering entering new markets, it's important to evaluate which approach aligns best with your business goals, resources, and capabilities. Here are factors to consider when evaluating the right approach:

a. **Market Analysis:** Assess market size and growth potential, competition level, cost of entry, and compatibility with your existing products, services, and brand positioning.

b. **Organizational Capabilities:** Consider the availability of resources, distribution networks, and customer support infrastructure.

c. **Feasibility:** Determine the feasibility of each approach based on your business's unique characteristics and strengths.

By conducting a comprehensive analysis, you can identify the approach that offers the greatest potential for success.

In the next sections of this chapter, we will explore the benefits and challenges associated with market expansion and diversification, provide insights on conducting market analysis, developing market entry strategies, and adapting to local market dynamics. Real-life examples and case studies of businesses that have successfully entered new markets will also be shared to inspire and guide you on your own journey. So, keep reading to gain valuable knowledge and practical guidance that will empower you to make informed decisions and drive your business growth through successful market expansion.

Section 3: Exploring the Benefits and Challenges of Diversification

In this section, we will delve into the concept of diversification as a strategy for business growth. If you're new to the topic, diversification involves expanding the range of products or services offered by your business. This strategic approach enables you to tap into new markets, meet evolving customer demands, and seize fresh opportunities. Let's explore the benefits, challenges, and key considerations of diversification to help you make informed decisions and guide your business toward success.

1. **Understanding Diversification as a Growth Strategy**

    Diversification is an essential growth strategy that allows businesses to expand their offerings beyond their existing product or service lines. By diversifying, you can extend your reach, cater to different customer segments, and capitalize on emerging trends. This strategic expansion enables your business to reduce its reliance on a single product or market, thereby minimizing risks and ensuring long-term sustainability.

    Remember in the previous section, diversification can take various forms. Additionally, diversification involves:

a. **Product Diversification:** This involves introducing new products or variations of existing ones. For instance, a clothing brand might diversify its product line by offering accessories or footwear.

b. **Service Diversification**: If your business primarily offers services, diversification can entail expanding into new service offerings. For example, a digital marketing agency might diversify by adding website development or social media management services.

c. **Industry Diversification**: Industry diversification involves entering new industries or sectors unrelated to your current business. This strategic move enables you to explore entirely different markets and capitalize on emerging opportunities.

2. **The Benefits of Diversification**

Diversification offers several strategic benefits for businesses:

- *Risk Mitigation:* By diversifying your offerings, you can reduce dependence on a single product or market. This strategy helps safeguard your business from potential disruptions, changes in customer preferences, or economic downturns. If one product or market faces challenges, other diversified segments can provide stability and mitigate risks.

- *Market Expansion:* Diversification allows you to tap into new customer segments and markets. By offering a broader range of products or services, you can attract new customers who may have different needs, preferences, or buying behaviors. This expanded customer base enhances your growth potential and revenue streams.

- *Competitive Advantage:* Diversification enables you to differentiate your business from competitors. By offering unique and complementary products or services, you can stand out in the market and provide additional value to your customers. This competitive advantage strengthens your market position and enhances customer loyalty.

3. **Challenges and Considerations**

While diversification can bring significant benefits, it's important to be aware of the challenges and considerations involved:

   a. **Market Research:** Conduct thorough market research to understand the target market for your new products or services. Assess customer needs, competition, market trends, and potential demand to ensure the viability of your diversification efforts.

   b. **Resource Allocation:** Diversification requires allocating resources effectively. Evaluate whether your business has the necessary capabilities, expertise, and resources to support the new offerings. Adequate staffing, production capacity, and operational capabilities are essential for successful diversification.

   c. **Brand Image and Reputation:** Consider the impact of diversification on your brand image and reputation. Ensure that the new offerings align with your brand values and do not dilute the quality or perception of your existing products or services.

4. **Developing a Diversification Strategy**

To successfully implement a diversification strategy, consider the following steps:

a. **Conduct a SWOT Analysis:** Evaluate your business's strengths, weaknesses, opportunities, and threats. Identify the areas where diversification can maximize your strengths and capitalize on market opportunities.

b. **Market Analysis:** Analyze the target market for your diversified offerings. Understand the market size, growth potential, competition, and customer needs to ensure a favorable market environment.

c. **Product Development and Marketing:** Develop a comprehensive product development plan to create new offerings or adapt existing ones. Craft a marketing strategy that effectively communicates the unique value of your diversified offerings to the target market.

5. **Real-Life Examples**

To provide practical insights, let's explore real-life examples of successful diversification strategies:

- Apple:

  Originally known for its personal computers, Apple successfully diversified into various product categories such as smartphones, tablets, wearables, and digital services. This diversification has propelled Apple's growth and positioned the company as a leader in multiple technology sectors.

- Amazon:

Initially an online bookstore, Amazon diversified its offerings to include a wide range of products and services, such as e-readers, cloud computing, streaming services, and smart devices. This diversification has fueled Amazon's expansion and established its presence as a global e-commerce and technology giant.

By studying these examples and understanding their strategic approaches to diversification, you can gain valuable insights to apply to your own business.

In the subsequent sections of this chapter, we will provide further guidance on conducting market analysis, developing entry strategies, and adapting to local market dynamics. Real-life case studies and examples of businesses that have successfully diversified their offerings will be shared to inspire and guide you in your own diversification journey. So, keep reading to gain valuable knowledge and practical guidance that will empower you to make informed decisions and drive your business growth through successful diversification.

Section 4: Market Analysis, Entry Strategies, and Adaptation to Local Market Dynamics

In this section, we will delve into the crucial aspects of market analysis, developing market entry strategies, and adapting to local market dynamics. If you are new to these topics, this section will provide you with the necessary insights and guidance to effectively expand your business into new markets. By understanding the importance of market analysis and implementing appropriate entry strategies, you can position your business for success in unfamiliar territories.

1. **Market Analysis: Understanding the Landscape**

Before entering a new market, conducting a comprehensive market analysis is essential. Market analysis involves gathering and evaluating data related to the target market's size, growth potential, competitive landscape, customer preferences, and local regulations. This analysis will provide you with valuable insights to make informed decisions and tailor your business strategies accordingly.

To conduct a thorough market analysis, consider the following steps:

a. **Identify Target Market:** Define your target market based on demographics, psychographics, and other relevant factors. Determine the size, growth rate, and characteristics of the market.

b. **Competitor Analysis:** Identify the key competitors in the target market and analyze their strengths, weaknesses, market share, pricing strategies, and customer perception. This analysis will help you identify opportunities for differentiation and competitive advantages.

c. **Customer Analysis:** Gain insights into the target market's preferences, needs, purchasing behaviors, and cultural considerations. Understand the local customer base to effectively position your products or services and tailor your marketing efforts.

d. **Regulatory and Legal Considerations:** Familiarize yourself with the local regulations, licensing requirements, and legal frameworks that govern business operations in the target market. Complying with local laws is crucial for successful market entry.

By conducting a comprehensive market analysis, you can make informed decisions about entering the market and develop strategies that resonate with the local customer base.

2. **Market Entry Strategies: Choosing the Right Approach**

Once you have conducted a market analysis, it's essential to select the most suitable market entry strategy for your business. Different market entry strategies exist, each with its own advantages and considerations. Here are a few common strategies to consider:

a. **Exporting:** Selling products or services directly to customers in the target market from your home country.

b. **Licensing and Franchising:** Granting licenses to local businesses to produce or sell your products or services, or establishing franchise partnerships.

c. **Joint Ventures and Strategic Partnerships:** Collaborating with local companies to enter the market together and leverage their knowledge, resources, and distribution networks.

d. **Direct Investment:** Establishing a physical presence in the target market through subsidiary operations, manufacturing facilities, or sales offices.

The choice of market entry strategy depends on various factors, including market characteristics, regulatory considerations, resource availability, and risk tolerance. Evaluate each strategy considering your specific business goals, capabilities, and the target market's dynamics to make an informed decision.

3. **Adapting to Local Market Dynamics**

Successful market entry requires adapting to the local market dynamics and meeting the unique needs and preferences of the target market. Here are some key considerations for adapting to local market dynamics:

a. **Cultural Relevance:** Understand the local culture, customs, traditions, and values. Adapt your marketing messages, branding, and customer experiences to resonate with the target market.

b. **Pricing and Competitive Strategies:** Evaluate local pricing norms, competitive landscape, and customer expectations to develop pricing strategies that are both competitive and profitable.

c. **Distribution and Supply Chain:** Establish efficient distribution networks and partnerships with local suppliers and logistics providers to ensure timely delivery and meet local demand.

d. **Marketing and Promotion:** Utilize local marketing channels, influencers, and advertising platforms that are popular and effective in the target market. Tailor your marketing campaigns to align with local preferences and communication styles.

e. **Customer Service and Support:** Offer exceptional customer service, considering the local expectations and communication preferences. Train your customer support teams to cater to the target market effectively.

By adapting to local market dynamics, you can gain a competitive edge, build strong customer relationships, and establish a solid presence in the new market.

In the subsequent sections of this chapter, we will further explore real-life case studies and examples of businesses that successfully entered new markets. By examining their strategies, challenges, and outcomes, you will gain practical insights and inspiration for your own market expansion efforts. So, continue reading to gain valuable knowledge and practical guidance that will empower you to navigate market analysis, develop effective entry strategies, and adapt to local market dynamics.

Section 5: Case Studies of Successful and Unsuccessful Market Expansion and Diversification

In this section, we will explore a mix of real-life case studies that showcase both successful and unsuccessful attempts at market expansion and diversification. By examining these examples, you will gain valuable insights into the factors that contribute to success as well as the pitfalls to avoid. These case studies will provide practical lessons for readers who are considering market expansion or diversification strategies for their own businesses.

1. **Successful Market Expansion Case Studies**

   - Starbucks:

     Starbucks, the renowned coffeehouse chain, successfully expanded its market from a single store to a global brand. Through strategic market expansion, Starbucks established a strong presence in over 80 countries. The company carefully analyzed local cultures, customized store designs, and localized marketing campaigns to create unique experiences for customers in each market. This approach allowed Starbucks to capture diverse customer segments and become a globally recognized brand.

- Netflix:

  Originally a DVD rental service, Netflix transformed its business model and achieved successful market expansion through digital streaming. By recognizing the changing preferences of consumers, Netflix shifted its focus to streaming video content. This strategic move enabled the company to cater to a global audience, delivering a vast library of movies and TV shows. By investing in original content and leveraging data-driven recommendations, Netflix became a dominant player in the streaming industry.

2. **Unsuccessful Diversification Case Studies**

- Blockbuster:

  Blockbuster, once a dominant player in the video rental industry, failed to adapt to the rise of digital streaming services. The company resisted embracing online rental and streaming options, which led to its decline. Blockbuster's failure to diversify its offerings and adapt to changing market dynamics serves as a cautionary tale about the importance of staying agile and responsive to evolving customer preferences.

- Kodak:

  Kodak, a renowned name in photography, struggled to transition from traditional film to digital imaging.

Despite being an early pioneer in digital photography technology, Kodak failed to fully embrace the digital revolution. The company's inability to adapt to market trends and leverage emerging technologies resulted in a decline in market share and eventual bankruptcy. Kodak's story highlights the importance of innovation, adaptability, and staying ahead of disruptive changes in the market.

By examining both successful and unsuccessful case studies of market expansion and diversification, you can gain a comprehensive understanding of the challenges, risks, and critical factors that can influence business growth and sustainability. Successful market expansion case studies provide valuable insights and inspiration for entering new markets, while unsuccessful diversification case studies shed light on the potential pitfalls and mistakes to avoid when diversifying offerings. Learning from both triumphs and failures will help you make more informed decisions and develop effective strategies for your own market expansion and diversification efforts.

Conclusion

In this chapter, we explored the strategies of market expansion and diversification as powerful tools for driving business growth. We discussed the concept of market expansion, which involves entering new markets beyond your current customer base or geographic reach. We also delved into diversification, which entails expanding the range of products or services your business offers. Throughout the chapter, we provided valuable insights, practical guidance, and real-life case studies to help you understand and implement these strategies effectively.

Market expansion offers opportunities to tap into new customer segments and regions, opening avenues for growth and revenue generation. By conducting thorough market research, tailoring your offerings, and strategically positioning your business, you can successfully expand into new markets. Whether it's geographical expansion or targeting new customer segments, choosing the right approach is essential for success.

Diversification, on the other hand, allows you to reduce reliance on a single product or market and seize new opportunities. By offering new products or services, related or unrelated to your existing offerings, you can cater to evolving customer demands and explore different market segments. We discussed various forms of diversification, including horizontal, vertical, and conglomerate, and emphasized the importance of market analysis, resource allocation, and brand alignment when implementing a diversification strategy.

Throughout the chapter, we highlighted the strategic importance of market expansion and diversification, such as increased market share, risk mitigation, and adaptability to market changes. We also examined real-life examples of successful and unsuccessful market expansion and diversification strategies employed by well-known companies, providing valuable lessons and insights.

To successfully implement market expansion and diversification strategies, we emphasized the need for comprehensive market analysis, sound entry strategies, and adaptation to local market dynamics. By understanding the landscape, choosing the right market entry approach, and adapting your business to local preferences, you can position yourself for success in new markets.

As we conclude this chapter, we hope that the knowledge, insights, and practical guidance provided have equipped you with the necessary tools to embark on your own market expansion and diversification journey. By leveraging these strategies effectively, you can drive sustainable growth, mitigate risks, and capitalize on new opportunities. Stay inspired, be open to innovation, and continue learning from both successful and unsuccessful cases to refine your strategies and achieve long-term business success.

Chapter 4: Effective Marketing and Customer Retention for Business Growth

—◇—

Introduction

In today's competitive business landscape, effective marketing plays a crucial role in driving business growth and acquiring new customers. A well-crafted marketing strategy, coupled with customer retention initiatives, can fuel your business's success and help you stay ahead of the competition. In this chapter, we will explore the significance of effective marketing and customer retention, provide guidance on developing a comprehensive marketing strategy, delve into various marketing channels and tactics, and showcase real-world examples of businesses that have achieved growth through successful marketing efforts. Let's dive in and discover how you can leverage marketing to propel your business forward.

Section 1: The Importance of Effective Marketing

In this section, we will explore why effective marketing is crucial for driving business growth and acquiring new customers. For readers who are new to the concept of marketing, this section will provide a comprehensive understanding of its significance and how it can benefit their business. Here are some key reasons why effective marketing is important:

1. **Building Brand Awareness:** Marketing helps create brand awareness by introducing your brand to your target audience and increasing its visibility in the market. It allows you to communicate your unique value proposition and make your brand familiar and recognizable.

2. **Acquiring New Customers:** Through strategic marketing efforts, you can identify and understand your target audience's needs, preferences, and pain points. By tailoring your marketing messages and offerings to resonate with them, you increase the likelihood of attracting the right customers who are most likely to convert and become loyal patrons.

3. **Communicating Value:** Effective marketing enables you to communicate the benefits and advantages of your products or services to your target audience. It allows you to address their specific problems or desires and demonstrate how your offerings meet their needs and enhance their lives.

4. **Establishing Trust and Credibility:** By consistently delivering compelling marketing messages and providing value to your audience, you build trust and credibility. This fosters strong relationships with your customers and encourages repeat business and referrals.

To embark on effective marketing, it's crucial to develop a deep understanding of your target audience. Here's how you can do that:

- **Conduct Market Research**: Identify your target audience's demographics, psychographics, and buying behaviors. Understand their preferences, motivations, and pain points.

- **Segment Your Audience:** Divide your target audience into distinct segments based on their characteristics and needs. This allows you to tailor your marketing efforts to each segment more effectively.

- **Craft Compelling Messages:** Use the insights from your market research to create targeted marketing messages that resonate with each segment of your audience. Highlight the unique benefits and value your products or services offer.

By investing in marketing strategies and tactics that align with your business goals and resonate with your audience, you can position your business for success in a competitive marketplace. The subsequent sections of this chapter will provide you with comprehensive guidance on developing a robust marketing strategy, exploring various marketing channels and tactics, implementing customer retention strategies, and showcasing real-world examples of businesses that have achieved growth through effective marketing. So, continue reading to gain valuable insights and practical guidance that will empower you to drive your business forward through strategic marketing initiatives.

Section 2: Developing a Comprehensive Marketing Strategy

In this section, we will discuss the key elements of developing a comprehensive marketing strategy that encompasses branding, messaging, and positioning. If you're new to marketing or looking to enhance your existing strategy, understanding these components is crucial for creating a strong foundation to attract and engage your target audience.

Let's explore each aspect in more detail and provide guidance on how to develop an effective marketing strategy:

1. **Branding**

   Branding is the process of creating a unique and memorable identity for your business in the minds of your target audience. It encompasses various elements, including your brand name, logo, colors, typography, and overall visual identity. Effective branding goes beyond aesthetics and reflects your business's values, personality, and the promise you make to your customers. Here's how you can develop a strong brand identity:

   a. Define Your Brand Identity: Start by defining your brand's mission, vision, values, and unique selling proposition (USP). Understand what sets your business apart from competitors and how you want to be perceived by your target audience.

   b. Create a Compelling Visual Identity: Design a visually appealing logo, choose a color palette that reflects your brand's personality, and select appropriate typography that aligns with your brand's tone. Consistency across all visual elements is essential for building brand recognition.

   c. Craft Your Brand Voice: Define your brand's tone of voice, which represents the style and way your brand communicates with your audience. Whether it's professional, friendly, playful, or authoritative, consistency in your brand voice helps build brand recognition and strengthens brand identity.

2. Messaging

Messaging involves crafting compelling and persuasive communication that resonates with your target audience. It includes the language, tone, and content that you use to convey your brand's value and offerings. Effective messaging captures the attention of your audience, communicates your unique selling points, and motivates them to act. Here's how to develop impactful messaging:

  a. **Identify Your Target Audience: Gain** a deep understanding of your target audience's demographics, psychographics, pain points, and aspirations. This knowledge will help you tailor your messages to their specific needs and motivations.

  b. **Highlight Your Unique Selling Points (USPs):** Identify the key features, benefits, or qualities that differentiate your products or services from competitors. These USPs form the foundation of your messaging and should be consistently communicated across your marketing materials.

  c. **Craft Clear and Compelling Copy:** Write concise and engaging copy that effectively communicates the value and benefits of your offerings. Focus on addressing the pain points of your audience and showcasing how your products or services solve their problems or fulfill their desires.

3. Positioning

Positioning is the process of establishing how your brand is perceived in the marketplace relative to competitors. It involves differentiating your brand and creating a unique position in the minds of your target audience. Effective positioning helps you stand out from the competition and connects with the specific needs and desires of your audience. Here are steps to develop a strong positioning strategy:

a. **Conduct Competitive Analysis:** Understand your competitors' strengths, weaknesses, market positioning, and target audience. This analysis will help you identify gaps and opportunities for positioning your brand uniquely.

b. **Determine Your Value Proposition:** Define the unique value that your brand offers to customers. Consider the benefits, solutions, or experiences that your products or services provide and articulate them clearly to establish your position in the market.

c. **Target Market Segmentation:** Identify specific segments within your target audience that align with your brand's value proposition. By targeting these segments, you can tailor your messaging and positioning to resonate with their specific needs and preferences.

Developing a comprehensive marketing strategy requires aligning your branding, messaging, and positioning to create a cohesive and compelling story for your target audience. By defining your brand identity, crafting impactful messaging, and establishing a unique market position, you can effectively communicate your brand's value and differentiate yourself from competitors.

In the subsequent sections of this chapter, we will explore various marketing channels and tactics, delve into customer retention strategies, and provide real-world examples and case studies of businesses that have achieved growth through effective marketing. So, keep reading to gain valuable insights and practical guidance that will empower you to develop a robust marketing strategy and drive your business forward.

Section 3: Exploring Various Marketing Channels and Tactics

In this section, we will explore different marketing channels and tactics that can effectively reach and engage your target audience. Whether you're new to marketing or looking to expand your current strategies, understanding these channels and tactics is essential for maximizing your reach and driving business growth. Let's delve into each one in more detail and provide clear guidance on how to leverage them effectively:

1. **Digital Marketing:**

   Digital marketing refers to the use of digital channels and technologies to promote your products or services. It has become increasingly important in today's digital age, where consumers spend a significant amount of time online.

   Here are some key digital marketing channels and tactics:

   a. **Search Engine Optimization (SEO):** SEO involves optimizing your website and content to rank higher in search engine results. By using relevant keywords, creating high-quality content, and improving website structure, you can increase your visibility and attract organic traffic.

   b. **Pay-Per-Click Advertising (PPC):** PPC advertising allows you to display targeted ads on search engine results pages or other websites. You only pay when someone clicks on your ad, making it a cost-effective way to drive traffic to your website and generate leads.

c. **Email Marketing:** Email marketing involves sending targeted emails to your subscribers to nurture relationships, promote products or services, and drive conversions. By delivering personalized and valuable content, you can build customer loyalty and increase sales.

d. **Content Marketing:** Content marketing focuses on creating and distributing valuable and relevant content to attract and engage your target audience. It can include blog posts, articles, videos, infographics, and more. By providing informative and valuable content, you can establish your brand as a trusted authority and attract potential customers.

2. **Social Media Marketing**

Social media marketing involves utilizing social media platforms to connect and engage with your target audience. It allows you to build brand awareness, foster customer relationships, and drive website traffic.

Here are some popular social media channels and tactics:

a. **Facebook:** With billions of active users, Facebook offers a wide range of targeting options and advertising formats. It's an effective platform for building brand presence, promoting products or services, and engaging with your audience through posts, comments, and messages.

b. **Instagram:** Known for its visual appeal, Instagram is ideal for businesses that can showcase their products or services through compelling images and videos. It's a great platform for building brand identity, engaging with influencers, and reaching a younger demographic.

c. **Twitter:** Twitter is a fast-paced platform that allows you to share short and concise messages, updates, and promotions. It's effective for real-time engagement, customer support, and reaching a broader audience through trending hashtags.

d. **LinkedIn:** LinkedIn is a professional networking platform that can be leveraged for B2B marketing. It allows you to connect with industry professionals, share thought leadership content, and promote your business to a targeted professional audience.

3. **Content Marketing**

Content marketing involves creating and distributing valuable content to attract and engage your target audience. It focuses on providing relevant and informative content that addresses the needs and interests of your audience.

Here are some content marketing tactics:

a. **Blogging:** Maintaining a blog on your website allows you to regularly publish articles, guides, and other educational content. It helps establish your brand as an industry expert, improves search engine visibility, and attracts organic traffic.

b. **Video Marketing:** Videos are highly engaging and shareable content formats. Creating videos that showcase your products, provide tutorials, or share industry insights can help increase brand awareness and engagement.

c. **Infographics:** Infographics present information in a visually appealing and easily digestible format. They can be shared on social media, embedded in blog posts, or used in presentations to convey complex information in a concise and attractive manner.

d. **Webinars and Podcasts:** Hosting webinars or creating podcasts allows you to share valuable insights, conduct interviews, and interact with your audience in a more interactive and engaging format. It positions your brand as a thought leader and provides valuable content for your audience.

4. **Partnerships and Collaborations**

Partnerships and collaborations involve working with other businesses or influencers to expand your reach and tap into new audiences.

Here's how you can leverage partnerships effectively:

a. **Influencer Marketing:** Collaborating with influencers who have a strong following in your target market allows you to leverage their reach and credibility. By partnering with influencers, you can promote your products or services to their audience and gain exposure.

b. **Co-marketing:** Partnering with complementary businesses that share a similar target audience can be mutually beneficial. By combining your marketing efforts, you can reach a wider audience and create synergistic marketing campaigns.

c. **Affiliate Marketing:** Affiliate marketing involves partnering with affiliates who promote your products or services in exchange for a commission.

This allows you to leverage their marketing efforts and expand your customer base.

By exploring and leveraging these various marketing channels and tactics, you can effectively reach and engage your target audience. It's important to understand your audience, set clear objectives, and measure the effectiveness of each channel to optimize your marketing strategy. In the subsequent sections of this chapter, we will discuss customer retention strategies and share real-world examples and case studies of businesses that have achieved growth through effective marketing and customer retention. So, continue reading to gain valuable insights and practical guidance that will empower you to implement successful marketing campaigns and drive your business forward.

Section 4: Hiring, Training, and Developing a High-Performing Team

In this section, we will discuss the importance of building a high-performing team to support business expansion. Hiring the right talent, providing effective training, and fostering continuous development are crucial for driving growth and achieving long-term success. Whether you're a business owner or a manager responsible for building a team, understanding these principles is essential for creating a productive and motivated workforce. Let's explore each aspect in more detail and provide actionable tips for hiring, training, and developing a high-performing team:

1. Hiring the Right Talent

Finding and hiring the right individuals for your team is the foundation of building a high-performing workforce. Here are some tips to help you hire the right talent:

a. **Define Job Roles and Requirements:** Clearly define the roles and responsibilities for each position you're hiring for. Identify the skills, qualifications, and experience necessary for success in those roles.

b. **Conduct Thorough Interviews:** During the interview process, ask behavioral and situational questions to assess candidates' skills, problem-solving abilities, and cultural fit. Use structured interviews and involve multiple interviewers to ensure a comprehensive evaluation.

c. **Assess Cultural Fit:** Consider the values, attitudes, and work style that align with your company culture. Look for candidates who demonstrate a strong fit and share your organization's core values.

d. **Consider Diversity and Inclusion:** Encourage diversity and inclusion in your hiring process to foster a more inclusive and innovative team. Ensure your hiring practices promote equal opportunities for candidates from different backgrounds.

2. **Providing Effective Training**

Once you have hired the right talent, it's important to provide effective training to equip them with the necessary skills and knowledge for their roles. Here's how you can provide effective training:

a. **Create a Structured Onboarding Program:** Develop a comprehensive onboarding program that introduces new hires to the company culture, values, and processes. Provide them with the necessary resources, tools, and information to quickly integrate into their roles.

b. **Offer Role-Specific Training:** Provide job-specific training to ensure employees have a clear understanding of their responsibilities and expectations. This can include technical training, product knowledge, and skill development programs tailored to each role.

c. **Implement Ongoing Learning and Development:** Foster a culture of continuous learning by offering ongoing training and development opportunities. This can include workshops, seminars, online courses, mentorship programs, and cross-functional projects.

d. **Encourage Knowledge Sharing:** Create platforms and opportunities for employees to share knowledge and best practices with each other. This can be through team meetings, internal newsletters, or online collaboration tools.

3. **Fostering Continuous Development**

To maintain a high-performing team, it's important to foster continuous development and growth. Here are some strategies to promote ongoing development:

a. **Set Clear Performance Expectations:** Define clear performance expectations and provide regular feedback to employees. Set measurable goals and provide constructive feedback to help them improve and grow.

b. **Encourage Skill Expansion:** Identify areas where employees can expand their skill sets and encourage them to take on new challenges and responsibilities. Provide support and resources for employees to develop new skills that align with their career goals.

c. **Offer Career Development Opportunities:** Provide opportunities for career advancement within your organization. This can include promotions, lateral moves, and special projects that allow employees to develop new skills and gain valuable experiences.

d. **Support Personal Growth:** Recognize and support employees' personal growth and well-being. Encourage work-life balance, offer flexible work arrangements, and provide resources for personal development outside of work.

By hiring the right talent, providing effective training, and fostering continuous development, you can build a high-performing team that supports business expansion. Remember to create a positive work environment, encourage open communication, and recognize and reward employee contributions. In the subsequent sections of this chapter, we will discuss customer retention strategies and share real-world examples and case studies of businesses that have achieved growth through effective marketing and customer retention. So, continue reading to gain valuable insights and practical guidance that will empower you to build and develop a high-performing team that drives your business forward.

Section 5: Customer Retention Strategies

In this section, we will delve into the importance of customer retention and explore various strategies to keep your customers engaged, satisfied, and loyal to your business. Customer retention is essential for sustainable growth and long-term success. By focusing on building strong relationships with your existing customers, you can maximize their lifetime value and foster brand advocacy. Whether you're a small business owner or a marketing professional, understanding customer retention strategies is crucial for driving business growth. Let's explore each strategy in more detail and provide actionable guidance:

1. **Implementing Loyalty Programs**

   Loyalty programs are a popular customer retention strategy that rewards customers for their repeat business and encourages them to continue engaging with your brand. Here's how you can implement an effective loyalty program:

   a. **Define the Program Structure:** Determine the rewards, points system, and tiers for your loyalty program. Consider offering discounts, exclusive perks, freebies, or personalized experiences based on customer preferences.

   b. **Make it Easy to Participate:** Ensure that your loyalty program is easy to understand, access, and participate in. Simplify the sign-up process, provide clear instructions, and offer multiple ways for customers to earn and redeem rewards.

   c. **Personalize the Experience:** Tailor your loyalty program to meet the individual preferences and behaviors of your customers. Use customer data and insights to deliver personalized offers and rewards that align with their interests.

d. **Regularly Communicate and Engage:** Keep your customers informed about their loyalty program status, new rewards, and exclusive offers through regular communication channels. Engage with them through targeted email campaigns, SMS notifications, or app notifications.

2. Providing Personalized Experiences

Personalization is key to enhancing customer satisfaction and retention. By tailoring your interactions and experiences to each customer's preferences, you can create a more meaningful connection. Here's how you can provide personalized experiences:

a. **Collect and Utilize Customer Data:** Gather relevant customer data through various touchpoints, such as purchase history, browsing behavior, and demographic information. Use this data to understand their preferences and deliver personalized experiences.

b. **Customize Product Recommendations:** Leverage customer data and AI-powered algorithms to offer personalized product recommendations based on their past purchases, browsing history, or similar customer preferences.

c. **Tailor Communication and Messaging:** Craft personalized communication messages that address customers by their name and provide relevant offers or recommendations based on their preferences. Use automation tools to deliver personalized email campaigns or personalized website content.

d. **Offer Customization Options:** Provide customers with the ability to customize products or services based on their individual needs or preferences. This could include customization of product features, packaging, or service options.

3. **Delivering Exceptional Customer Service**

    Exceptional customer service is a crucial element of customer retention. By providing outstanding support and addressing customer needs promptly, you can enhance their satisfaction and loyalty. Here are some tips for delivering exceptional customer service:

    a. **Train and Empower Customer Support Teams:** Invest in training your customer support teams to ensure they have the necessary skills and knowledge to provide excellent service. Empower them to make decisions and resolve customer issues efficiently.

    b. **Implement Omnichannel Support**: Offer customer support through multiple channels, such as phone, email, live chat, or social media. Ensure a seamless experience across channels and respond promptly to customer inquiries or complaints.

    c. **Personalize Customer Interactions:** Train your customer support teams to engage with customers on a personal level. Use customer data to understand their history and preferences, and reference this information during interactions.

    d. **Proactively Seek Customer Feedback:** Regularly seek feedback from customers to understand their needs and identify areas for improvement. This can be done through surveys, feedback forms, or customer review platforms. Act on customer feedback to continuously enhance your customer service.

By implementing loyalty programs, providing personalized experiences, and delivering exceptional customer service, you can effectively retain your customers and foster long-term loyalty. Remember to regularly evaluate the success of your retention strategies by measuring key metrics such as customer retention rate, repeat purchase rate, and customer satisfaction scores.

In the subsequent sections of this chapter, we will share real-world examples and case studies of businesses that have achieved growth through effective marketing and customer retention. So, keep reading to gain valuable insights and practical guidance that will empower you to implement these strategies in your own business and drive customer loyalty and growth.

Section 6: Real-World Examples of Businesses Achieving Growth through Effective Marketing and Customer Retention

In this section, we will explore real-world examples and case studies of businesses that have achieved growth through their effective marketing strategies and customer retention efforts. These examples will provide you with valuable insights and inspiration for implementing similar tactics in your own business. Let's dive into two noteworthy success stories:

1. **Nike:**

   Nike is a powerhouse in the sports apparel and footwear industry, known for its iconic branding and effective marketing campaigns. Nike's marketing strategy revolves around inspiring and empowering athletes of all levels. The company strategically partners with high-profile athletes, sponsors major sporting events, and produces compelling advertisements that resonate with its target audience. Nike's commitment to customer engagement and retention is evident through its NikePlus membership program, which offers exclusive benefits, personalized recommendations, and access to unique experiences.

Nike's success can be attributed to several key factors:

a. Branding and Messaging: Nike has built a strong brand identity centered around inspiration, empowerment, and athleticism. The company's iconic "Just Do It" slogan has become synonymous with motivation and determination. Nike's messaging consistently resonates with its target audience, inspiring them to push their limits and achieve their goals.

b. Partnerships: Nike strategically collaborates with high-profile athletes, sports teams, and influential figures in the sporting world. These partnerships not only enhance Nike's credibility and visibility but also create a strong emotional connection with consumers who aspire to be like their favorite athletes.

c. Compelling Advertising: Nike produces powerful and emotionally engaging advertisements that capture the spirit of sports and the passion of athletes. Their ads often tell inspiring stories, evoke emotions, and align with social and cultural movements, making them memorable and resonant with consumers.

d. NikePlus Membership Program: Nike's membership program, NikePlus, offers exclusive benefits to members, such as early access to new product releases, personalized recommendations, and invitations to special events. This program enhances customer loyalty by providing a personalized and rewarding experience for members.

2. **Sephora:**

Sephora, a renowned beauty retailer, has thrived through its customer-centric approach and innovative marketing strategies. The company emphasizes personalized experiences and education, allowing customers to explore products, receive expert advice, and try samples in-store. Sephora's Beauty Insider loyalty program offers exclusive perks, rewards, and personalized recommendations based on customers' preferences and purchase history.

Sephora's success can be attributed to several key factors:

a. **In-Store Experience:** Sephora provides a unique and immersive in-store experience where customers can discover and test a wide range of beauty products. The stores feature interactive displays, knowledgeable staff, and beauty services, creating a welcoming environment for customers to explore and experiment with different products.

b. **Personalized Recommendations:** Sephora utilizes customer data and preferences to provide personalized product recommendations. This customization enhances the shopping experience and makes customers feel understood and valued.

c. **Beauty Insider Loyalty Program:** Sephora's Beauty Insider program rewards customers with exclusive perks, access to limited-edition products, and personalized beauty advice. The program fosters customer loyalty by providing tangible benefits and creating a sense of community among members.

d. **Educational Content:** Sephora offers online and in-store beauty tutorials, tips, and how-to guides, empowering customers with knowledge and helping them make informed purchasing decisions. By providing educational content, Sephora positions itself as a trusted authority in the beauty industry.

These examples demonstrate how effective marketing and customer retention strategies can drive business growth and foster customer loyalty. By studying the approaches taken by Nike and Sephora, you can gain valuable insights into building a strong brand, creating compelling marketing campaigns, and implementing customer-centric initiatives.

In the subsequent sections of this chapter, we will provide further guidance on developing and implementing your own marketing strategies and customer retention initiatives. We will delve into the specifics of different marketing channels, explore digital marketing techniques, and discuss the importance of measuring and analyzing your marketing efforts. So, continue reading to gain practical guidance and inspiration that will empower you to achieve growth through effective marketing and customer retention strategies in your own business.

Conclusion

In this chapter, we delved into the importance of effective marketing and customer retention strategies for driving business growth. We explored various aspects of developing a comprehensive marketing strategy, including branding, messaging, and positioning. We also discussed different marketing channels and tactics, such as digital marketing, social media, content marketing, and partnerships. Furthermore, we examined customer retention strategies, including loyalty programs, personalized experiences, and exceptional customer service. Throughout the chapter, we provided real-world examples and case studies of businesses that achieved growth through their marketing and customer retention efforts.

Effective marketing is a crucial element in driving business growth and acquiring new customers. By developing a comprehensive marketing strategy that aligns with your business goals and target audience, you can create a strong brand identity, engage with your customers, and differentiate yourself from the competition. It is essential to leverage various marketing channels and tactics to reach your target audience effectively and maximize your marketing efforts.

Customer retention is equally important as acquiring new customers. By implementing strategies such as loyalty programs, personalized experiences, and exceptional customer service, you can cultivate long-term relationships with your existing customers, increase their loyalty, and drive repeat purchases. Building a strong customer retention strategy contributes to customer satisfaction, brand advocacy, and ultimately, sustainable business growth.

Throughout the chapter, we explored real-world examples of businesses that have achieved growth through effective marketing and customer retention strategies. Companies like Nike and Sephora demonstrated the power of branding, partnerships, personalized experiences, and loyalty programs in driving customer engagement and loyalty. These examples serve as inspiration and provide valuable insights into the successful implementation of marketing and customer retention strategies.

As we conclude this chapter, we hope that you have gained valuable knowledge and practical guidance that will empower you to develop and implement effective marketing strategies and customer retention initiatives in your own business. The key takeaway is to understand the importance of marketing as a driver of growth and the significance of building strong relationships with your customers. By continuously evolving your marketing strategies, adapting to market trends, and prioritizing customer satisfaction, you can position your business for long-term success.

In the next chapter, Chapter 5: Developing Strategic Partnerships, we will explore the role of strategic partnerships in fueling business growth and expansion. We will discuss different types of strategic partnerships, such as joint ventures, distribution agreements, or co-marketing initiatives. Additionally, we will provide guidance on identifying and selecting potential partners, negotiating partnerships, and managing collaborations. The chapter will delve into the benefits and challenges of strategic partnerships, including increased market reach, shared resources, and access to new capabilities. Real-life case studies and examples of businesses that have successfully developed and leveraged strategic partnerships will be shared to inspire and guide you on your partnership journey. So, continue reading to gain valuable insights and practical guidance that will empower you to harness the power of strategic partnerships for your business growth.

Chapter 5: Developing Strategic Partnerships

---◦◇◦---

Introduction

In this chapter, we will explore the significant role that strategic partnerships play in fueling business growth and expansion. We will discuss the various types of strategic partnerships, such as joint ventures, distribution agreements, or co-marketing initiatives, and examine their benefits and challenges. Additionally, we will provide guidance on how to identify and select potential partners, negotiate partnerships, and effectively manage collaborations. Throughout the chapter, we will include real-life case studies and examples of businesses that have successfully developed and leveraged strategic partnerships to inspire and guide you in your own partnership endeavors.

Section 1: The Role of Strategic Partnerships in Business Growth and Expansion

In this section, we will explore the essential role that strategic partnerships play in driving business growth and expansion. For readers who may be unfamiliar with the concept of strategic partnerships, we will provide a clear explanation and offer practical guidance on how to leverage them effectively.

1. **Strategic partnerships** are collaborative relationships established between two or more businesses with the purpose of achieving mutually beneficial goals. These

partnerships are built on the principle of combining resources, expertise, and capabilities to create value that surpasses what each business could achieve individually.

Let's explore some of the benefits strategic partnerships offer:

One of the primary benefits of strategic partnerships is the *ability to access new markets and customers*. By partnering with another company that has an established presence in a target market or customer segment, businesses can leverage their partner's distribution channels, customer base, and brand reputation to expand their reach and generate new sales opportunities. This access to a broader market can significantly accelerate business growth and increase revenue streams.

Additionally, strategic partnerships *enable businesses to enhance their competitive advantage*. By collaborating with complementary companies that possess expertise, technologies, or resources that align with their own strengths and strategic objectives, businesses can create unique value propositions that differentiate them from competitors. For example, a technology company may partner with a marketing agency to combine cutting-edge software solutions with effective marketing strategies, providing customers with a comprehensive and innovative offering.

Another key aspect of strategic partnerships is the *sharing of resources and capabilities*. By pooling together financial resources, infrastructure, intellectual property, or specialized knowledge, businesses can achieve economies of scale, reduce costs, and drive operational efficiencies. This sharing of resources allows each partner to leverage their collective strengths and overcome individual limitations, resulting in improved productivity and performance.

Strategic partnerships also offer **opportunities for innovation and learning**. Through collaborative efforts, businesses can exchange ideas, insights, and best practices, leading to the development of new products, services, or processes. This collaborative innovation fosters creativity, promotes continuous improvement, and enables businesses to stay at the forefront of their industries.

However, it's important to note that strategic partnerships come with their own set of challenges. Building and maintaining effective partnerships requires open communication, trust, and a shared vision. Businesses must carefully select partners who align with their values, objectives, and corporate culture to ensure a harmonious and productive collaboration. Additionally, clear expectations, responsibilities, and governance structures should be established through well-defined agreements to manage potential conflicts or misunderstandings.

To harness the benefits of strategic partnerships, businesses should consider the following guidance:

a. **Clearly define your business objectives:** Determine the specific goals you aim to achieve through a strategic partnership, such as expanding into new markets, accessing new technologies, or enhancing operational efficiencies. This clarity will guide your search for potential partners.

b. **Identify complementary businesses:** Look for companies that possess complementary capabilities, resources, or market presence that align with your business goals. Consider factors such as expertise, customer base, distribution channels, or intellectual property that can enhance your competitive advantage.

c. **Assess potential partners:** Conduct thorough due diligence to evaluate potential partners' reputation, financial stability, cultural fit, and track record of successful collaborations. Seek references, review case studies, and engage in discussions to ensure alignment and minimize risks.

d. **Establish clear communication and collaboration mechanisms:** Define communication channels, decision-making processes, and governance structures to facilitate effective collaboration. Regular meetings, joint planning sessions, and performance evaluations should be established to ensure alignment and monitor progress.

e. **Maintain open and transparent communication: Foster** a culture of trust and transparency by maintaining open lines of communication with your strategic partner. Encourage frequent dialogue, share information, and address any concerns or challenges promptly to build a strong and collaborative relationship.

By following these guidelines, businesses can harness the power of strategic partnerships to drive growth, access new markets, enhance their competitive advantage, and foster innovation. In the next sections of this chapter, we will explore different types of strategic partnerships and provide guidance on identifying and selecting potential partners, negotiating partnerships, and effectively managing collaborations. Additionally, we will share real-life examples and case studies of businesses that have successfully leveraged strategic partnerships to inspire and guide you on your own journey toward business growth and expansion.

Section 2: Exploring Different Types of Strategic Partnerships

In this section, we will delve into the various types of strategic partnerships that businesses can engage in to fuel their growth and expansion. For readers who may be unfamiliar with these partnership types, we will provide a comprehensive explanation and offer clear guidance on how each type can be utilized effectively.

1. **Joint Ventures**

   A joint venture is a strategic partnership where two or more businesses come together to form a new entity or venture with shared ownership and control. This type of partnership allows businesses to combine their resources, expertise, and market knowledge to pursue a specific opportunity or achieve a common goal. Joint ventures are commonly used when entering new markets, developing new products or services, or pooling resources for large-scale projects. By sharing risks, costs, and responsibilities, businesses can tap into new markets or undertake ventures that would be challenging or impractical to pursue individually.

   Guidance:

   a. Clearly define the objectives and scope of the joint venture.

   b. Establish a detailed agreement outlining the ownership structure, decision-making processes, and profit-sharing mechanisms.

    c.   Allocate roles and responsibilities to each partner based on their strengths and expertise.

    d.   Regularly communicate and collaborate with your joint venture partner to ensure alignment and success.

2. Distribution Agreements

Distribution agreements involve partnering with another business to distribute or sell your products or services. This type of partnership is particularly useful when entering new markets or expanding into different geographical regions. By leveraging the distribution channels and existing customer base of your partner, you can accelerate market penetration and reach a wider audience. Distribution agreements can take various forms, such as exclusive distribution, non-exclusive distribution, or selective distribution, depending on the level of control and exclusivity desired.

Guidance:

    a.   Identify potential distribution partners with a strong market presence and compatible customer base.

    b.   Define the terms of the agreement, including territory, duration, pricing, and marketing support.

    c.   Establish clear communication channels and reporting mechanisms to monitor sales performance and ensure mutual success.

    d.   Regularly assess the effectiveness of the distribution partnership and adapt strategies as needed.

3. Co-Marketing Initiatives

Co-marketing initiatives involve collaborating with another business to jointly promote and market products or services. This partnership leverages the complementary strengths, customer base, or marketing channels of both businesses to maximize brand exposure, reach new audiences, and drive sales. Co-marketing can take various forms, including joint advertising campaigns, co-branded products, or shared content marketing efforts. By combining marketing resources and tapping into each other's networks, businesses can generate greater visibility and engagement.

Guidance:

a. Identify partners with complementary target markets, brand values, and marketing capabilities.

b. Define the objectives, scope, and expected outcomes of the co-marketing initiative.

c. Develop a clear plan for joint marketing activities, such as creating co-branded content, organizing events, or running joint promotions.

d. Regularly evaluate the effectiveness of the co-marketing efforts and optimize strategies based on performance metrics and customer feedback.

Other types of strategic partnerships may include technology collaborations, research and development **partnerships, supplier partnerships**, or even **alliances with competitors** in certain cases. The specific type of partnership that best suits your business will depend on your objectives, industry, and available resources.

When exploring different types of strategic partnerships, it is essential to *consider the compatibility of values, goals, and capabilities between your business and potential partners.* Aligning your strategic objectives, establishing clear communication channels, and defining the roles and responsibilities of each partner are crucial for successful collaboration.

In the subsequent sections of this chapter, we will provide guidance on identifying and selecting potential partners, negotiating partnerships, and effectively managing collaborations. Additionally, we will share real-life examples and case studies of businesses that have achieved significant growth and expansion through different types of strategic partnerships. These examples will inspire and guide you in leveraging strategic partnerships to drive your own business growth and foster long-term success.

Section 3: Guidance on Identifying, Selecting, and Negotiating Partnerships

In this section, we will provide valuable guidance on how to effectively identify, select, and negotiate partnerships for your business. For readers who may be unfamiliar with this process, we will offer clear explanations and practical tips to help you navigate through these important stages successfully.

1. **Identifying Potential Partners**

   To begin the partnership journey, it is crucial to identify potential partners that align with your business goals, values, and strategic objectives. Here's how you can go about it:

   a. Conduct Market Research: Start by researching your industry and target market to identify businesses that complement your products, services, or target audience. Look for potential partners who have expertise, resources, or a market presence that can enhance your offerings or expand your reach.

b. Attend Industry Events and Networking: Participate in industry conferences, trade shows, and networking events to connect with potential partners. Engage in conversations, exchange ideas, and explore mutual interests. Building relationships and expanding your professional network can lead to promising partnership opportunities.

c. Seek Recommendations: Reach out to industry experts, mentors, or trusted colleagues for recommendations on potential partners. They may have insights into businesses that could be a good fit for collaboration or be able to connect you with relevant contacts.

2. Selecting the Right Partner

Once you have identified potential partners, the next step is to evaluate and select the partner that best aligns with your business objectives. Consider the following factors during the selection process:

a. **Compatibility:** Assess the compatibility of values, culture, and strategic vision between your business and potential partners. Look for alignment in terms of goals, target markets, and customer segments. A compatible partner will enhance the chances of a successful collaboration.

b. **Expertise and Resources:** Evaluate the expertise, resources, and capabilities that the potential partner brings to the table. Consider how their strengths complement your business and how they can contribute to the partnership's success.

c. **Track Record and Reputation:** Research the potential partner's track record, reputation, and past collaborations. Look for evidence of successful partnerships or business practices that align with your values and expectations.

d. **Communication and Trust:** Assess the communication style, responsiveness, and willingness to collaborate displayed by the potential partner. Building a foundation of trust and effective communication is crucial for a successful partnership.

3. **Negotiating Partnerships**

Negotiating a partnership agreement is a critical step in ensuring that both parties are clear on expectations, roles, and responsibilities. Here are some tips for successful partnership negotiations:

a. **Define Objectives and Expectations:** Clearly articulate the objectives, scope, and desired outcomes of the partnership. Ensure that both parties have a shared understanding of the partnership's purpose and the specific goals to be achieved.

b. **Establish Mutual Benefits:** Identify and communicate the mutual benefits that each partner will gain from the partnership. This could include increased market reach, shared resources, access to new capabilities, or cost savings.

c. **Collaborate on Terms and Conditions:** Collaboratively define the terms and conditions of the partnership agreement, including ownership structure, decision-making processes, profit sharing, intellectual property rights, and exit strategies. Seek legal counsel to ensure that the agreement is comprehensive, fair, and legally binding.

d. **Communication and Conflict Resolution:** Establish clear communication channels and protocols to facilitate ongoing collaboration. Develop strategies for conflict resolution and decision-making processes to address any challenges that may arise during the partnership.

4. **Managing Collaborations**

Once the partnership is established, effective management is crucial to ensure its success. Here are some tips for managing collaborations:

a. **Open and Transparent Communication:** Maintain regular and open communication with your partner. Keep each other informed about progress, challenges, and changes that may impact the partnership.

b. **Defined Roles and Responsibilities:** Clearly define the roles and responsibilities of each partner within the partnership. This will help ensure that tasks are completed efficiently and prevent confusion or duplication of efforts.

c. **Regular Evaluation and Feedback:** Continuously evaluate the partnership's performance and provide feedback to each other. Regularly assess whether the partnership is meeting its objectives and adjust as needed.

d. **Adaptability and Flexibility:** Remain adaptable and flexible to accommodate changes in the business landscape, market dynamics, or strategic objectives. Flexibility is key to sustaining a successful partnership over the long term.

By following these guidelines for identifying, selecting, negotiating, and managing partnerships, you can set a strong foundation for fruitful collaborations that contribute to your business growth and expansion. Remember, strategic partnerships have the potential to open new doors, expand market reach, and unlock valuable resources and capabilities that can propel your business to new heights of success.

Section 4: Managing Collaborations and Overcoming Challenges

In this section, we will delve into the important topic of managing strategic partnerships and overcoming the challenges that may arise during the collaborative process. For readers who may be unfamiliar with this area, we will provide a comprehensive understanding of the benefits and challenges associated with strategic partnerships. Additionally, we will offer clear guidance on how to effectively manage collaborations and address potential hurdles.

1. **Benefits of Strategic Partnerships**

Strategic partnerships offer numerous benefits that can significantly contribute to the growth and success of your business. Here are some key advantages:

   a. **Increased Market Reach:** Strategic partnerships allow you to tap into new markets and customer segments that may have been difficult to access independently. By leveraging the partner's existing customer base or distribution channels, you can expand your market reach and potentially gain a larger share of the market.

b. **Shared Resources:** Collaborating with a strategic partner enables you to pool resources, such as finances, technology, infrastructure, or expertise. This shared resource approach can provide cost savings, accelerate growth, and enhance operational efficiency.

c. **Access to New Capabilities:** Partnering with a business that has complementary capabilities or expertise can give you access to new knowledge, technologies, or skills. This can help you enhance your product/service offerings, improve operational processes, or innovate more effectively.

d. **Risk Mitigation:** Strategic partnerships can help mitigate risks by sharing the burden of investments, market uncertainties, or changing industry dynamics. By spreading risks across multiple parties, you can navigate challenges more effectively and ensure a more stable business environment.

2. **Challenges of Strategic Partnerships**

While strategic partnerships offer significant benefits, it's important to be aware of the potential challenges that may arise. Understanding these challenges can help you proactively address them and ensure the success of your collaborations. Here are some common challenges:

a. **Alignment of Goals and Values:** Ensuring alignment of goals, values, and strategic vision between partners is crucial for a successful collaboration.

Misalignment in these areas can lead to conflicts, misunderstandings, or incompatible business strategies.

b. **Communication and Decision-making: Effective** communication and decision-making processes are essential for smooth collaborations. Differences in communication styles, decision-making approaches, or information sharing can hinder progress and cause delays or misunderstandings.

c. **Power Dynamics:** Managing power dynamics within a partnership can be challenging, especially if there is a significant difference in size, resources, or influence between the partners. Balancing power and ensuring equitable participation can foster a healthy and productive collaborative environment.

d. **Resource Allocation and Dependencies:** Managing resources and dependencies can be complex in a partnership. Conflicts may arise when partners have varying expectations or commitments in terms of resource allocation or sharing. Clear agreements and effective resource management are essential to address these challenges.

e. **Trust and Relationship Building:** Building and maintaining trust between partners is crucial for a successful collaboration. Trust is the foundation upon which effective communication, cooperation, and shared decision-making are built. Building trust takes time and requires open communication, transparency, and consistent delivery on commitments.

3. **Strategies for Managing Collaborations and Overcoming Challenges**

To effectively manage strategic partnerships and address the challenges that may arise, consider the following strategies:

a. **Clear Communication and Expectations:** Establish clear lines of communication and set expectations from the beginning. Clearly articulate roles, responsibilities, and objectives to ensure mutual understanding and alignment.

b. **Trust-Building Activities:** Invest time and effort in relationship-building activities to foster trust and rapport between partners. Regularly engage in open and transparent communication, collaborate on joint initiatives, and celebrate milestones together.

c. **Collaboration Frameworks**: Develop collaborative frameworks that define decision-making processes, resource allocation, and conflict resolution mechanisms. Having clear guidelines in place helps manage expectations and ensures fairness and accountability.

d. **Regular Evaluation and Feedback:** Conduct regular evaluations of the partnership's progress and effectiveness. Encourage open feedback and constructive dialogue to address any concerns or challenges promptly.

e. **Flexibility and Adaptability:** Remain flexible and adaptable to accommodate changes in the business landscape or evolving partnership dynamics. Embrace a collaborative mindset and be open to adjusting strategies or approaches as needed.

f. **Mediation and Conflict Resolution:** Establish a mechanism for resolving conflicts or disagreements that may arise. Mediation or third-party facilitation can help address conflicts objectively and find mutually beneficial solutions.

By proactively managing collaborations and addressing challenges as they arise, you can foster a productive and mutually beneficial partnership. Remember, effective collaboration requires ongoing effort, open communication, and a commitment to nurturing the relationship for long-term success. Strategic partnerships have the potential to unlock growth opportunities, expand market reach, and enhance competitiveness, making them valuable assets for driving business growth and expansion.

Section 5: Case Studies of Successful Strategic Partnerships

In this section, we will delve into real-world examples and case studies of businesses that have successfully developed and leveraged strategic partnerships to drive growth and achieve their business objectives. These case studies will provide valuable insights into the practical application of strategic partnerships and demonstrate how businesses can benefit from collaborative efforts. Let's explore some inspiring examples:

1. **Nike and Apple**

   Nike, a leading sportswear brand, and Apple, a technology giant, formed a successful strategic partnership by integrating their products and services. The collaboration resulted in the development of Nike+, a platform that combined Nike's athletic footwear and apparel with Apple's iPod and later the iPhone. This partnership allowed Nike to leverage Apple's technology to enhance the running experience for its customers. Through the Nike+ platform, runners could track their performance, set goals, and connect with a community of like-minded individuals. This partnership not only improved the value proposition for Nike's customers but also opened new revenue streams and expanded market reach for both companies.

2. **Sephora and Pantone**

Sephora, a renowned beauty retailer, partnered with Pantone, a leading authority on color, to create a successful co-marketing initiative. The partnership resulted in the development of the "Color of the Year" campaign. Each year, Pantone selects a color that represents current trends and influences various industries, including fashion and beauty. Sephora capitalized on this by curating a collection of beauty products that align with the Color of the Year. Through joint marketing efforts, including in-store displays, online promotions, and social media campaigns, Sephora and Pantone created excitement and buzz around the color trend, driving customer engagement and sales. This strategic partnership allowed Sephora to position itself as a trendsetter in the beauty industry and leverage Pantone's expertise to offer exclusive and highly sought-after products.

3. **Spotify and Uber**

Spotify, a popular music streaming service, teamed up with Uber, a leading ride-sharing platform, to create an innovative partnership that enhanced the customer experience. Through this collaboration, Uber customers could connect their Spotify accounts and enjoy personalized music playlists during their rides. This integration created a seamless and enjoyable experience for passengers, allowing them to control the music playing in their Uber rides through the Spotify app. This partnership not only enhanced the value proposition for Uber passengers but also introduced Spotify to a broader audience and increased user engagement. By leveraging each other's platforms and customer bases, Spotify and Uber successfully differentiated themselves in their respective industries and provided a unique and memorable experience for their customers.

These case studies highlight the power of strategic partnerships in driving business growth and delivering enhanced value to customers. By aligning complementary strengths, leveraging each other's resources, and creating innovative offerings, these businesses were able to expand their market reach, differentiate themselves from competitors, and provide a seamless and engaging customer experience.

When exploring potential strategic partnerships for your own business, it's important to consider the industry landscape, complementary capabilities, shared objectives, and alignment of values. By studying successful case studies like the ones mentioned above, you can gain insights into effective partnership models, identify key success factors, and apply those lessons to your own strategic collaborations.

Remember, strategic partnerships are not one-size-fits-all, and it's essential to evaluate the unique needs and objectives of your business. By seeking out synergistic partnerships and nurturing collaborative relationships, you can unlock new growth opportunities, access additional resources and capabilities, and ultimately drive your business towards greater success.

Conclusion

In this chapter, we explored the world of strategic partnerships and their crucial role in fueling business growth and expansion.

We discussed various aspects of strategic partnerships, including their types, identification and selection, negotiation, and management. Additionally, we examined the benefits and challenges that come with forming strategic partnerships and shared real-world case studies of businesses that achieved success through effective collaborations.

Strategic partnerships have become increasingly important in today's interconnected and competitive business landscape. By joining forces with the right partners, businesses can tap into new markets, access shared resources, and leverage complementary capabilities to achieve their growth objectives. These partnerships offer opportunities for increased market reach, enhanced product offerings, improved customer experiences, and accelerated innovation.

When developing strategic partnerships, it is crucial to identify partners whose goals and values align with your own. Conduct thorough research and due diligence to find partners who bring complementary strengths, expertise, and customer bases to the table. Effective communication, trust, and mutual understanding are vital throughout the partnership's lifecycle.

Negotiating partnership agreements requires careful consideration of shared objectives, roles, responsibilities, and expectations. Clear and well-defined contractual terms should be established to ensure a mutually beneficial collaboration. Effective management of partnerships involves open communication, regular performance evaluation, and a commitment to addressing challenges and conflicts that may arise.

Throughout this chapter, we examined successful case studies of strategic partnerships, including Nike and Apple, Sephora and Pantone, and Spotify and Uber. These examples illustrated how businesses can leverage strategic collaborations to enhance their offerings, expand their market presence, and provide unique value propositions to their customers.

As you embark on your own journey of developing strategic partnerships, remember to assess the potential benefits and challenges specific to your industry and business objectives. Seek partners who bring complementary strengths, shared values, and a long-term vision for growth. By leveraging strategic partnerships, you can propel your business forward, unlock new opportunities, and create a competitive advantage in the marketplace.

In the next chapter, we will explore another crucial aspect of business growth: innovation. We will delve into strategies for fostering a culture of innovation, developing new products and services, and adapting to changing market dynamics. So, stay tuned for valuable insights and practical guidance to drive innovation within your organization.

Part 3: Cultivating Innovation and Adaptation

Chapter 6: Innovation and Adaptation for Growth

---•o◇o•---

Introduction

In today's fast-paced and ever-changing business landscape, the ability to innovate and adapt is crucial for driving growth and maintaining a competitive edge. In this chapter, we will explore the importance of innovation and adaptation in business, techniques for fostering a culture of innovation, identifying market trends, developing innovative products or services, and leveraging technology for business growth. Real-life examples and case studies will illustrate how businesses have successfully embraced innovation and adaptation to achieve sustainable growth.

Section 1: The Importance of Innovation and Adaptation in Driving Business Growth and Staying Competitive

In today's dynamic and rapidly evolving business landscape, the importance of innovation and adaptation cannot be overstated. In this section, we will explore why innovation and adaptation are crucial for driving business growth and staying competitive. Whether you are a business owner, entrepreneur, or aspiring professional, understanding the significance of innovation and adaptation is essential for your success. Let's delve deeper into this topic and discover why it matters.

1. **Driving Business Growth**

   Innovation and adaptation are key drivers of business growth. They enable companies to identify new opportunities, create unique value propositions, and differentiate themselves from competitors. By continuously innovating, businesses can develop new products, services, or business models that meet evolving customer needs and preferences. This not only attracts new customers but also helps in retaining existing ones, leading to increased market share and revenue growth.

2. **Staying Competitive**

   In a rapidly changing business environment, staying competitive is crucial for survival. Businesses that fail to innovate and adapt risk becoming obsolete or losing market relevance. By proactively embracing change, companies can anticipate market shifts, industry disruptions, and emerging trends. This allows them to stay ahead of the competition and respond effectively to new challenges. Innovation and adaptation help businesses remain agile, flexible, and responsive to customer demands, giving them a competitive edge.

3. **Meeting Customer Expectations**

   Customers today have higher expectations than ever before. They seek innovative solutions, personalized experiences, and convenience. By continuously innovating and adapting, businesses can meet and exceed customer expectations. Innovation allows for the development of products or services that address specific pain points and deliver enhanced value. Adaptation enables businesses to respond to changing customer preferences, market trends, and technological advancements, ensuring continued customer satisfaction and loyalty.

4. Seizing New Opportunities

Innovation and adaptation open doors to new opportunities. They allow businesses to explore untapped markets, expand into new customer segments, or diversify their offerings. By constantly seeking ways to improve and evolve, businesses can discover unmet needs, identify gaps in the market, and capitalize on emerging trends. This proactive approach to innovation and adaptation enables businesses to seize opportunities that may not be apparent to others, driving growth and competitive advantage.

5. Fostering Organizational Resilience

Innovation and adaptation build resilience within organizations. By embracing change and fostering a culture of innovation, businesses become more adaptable and responsive to external disruptions. They can quickly pivot their strategies, processes, and offerings in response to unforeseen events or market shifts. This resilience enables businesses to navigate challenges, overcome obstacles, and maintain long-term sustainability in an ever-changing business landscape.

To harness the power of innovation and adaptation, businesses should cultivate an environment that encourages creative thinking, embraces experimentation, and values continuous improvement. This involves fostering a culture of open communication, collaboration, and learning. Leaders should provide the necessary resources, support risk-taking, and recognize and reward innovative ideas and initiatives. By doing so, businesses can create a thriving ecosystem that drives innovation and adaptation at all levels.

In conclusion, innovation and adaptation are critical for driving business growth and staying competitive in today's fast-paced and dynamic business world. By embracing change, meeting customer expectations, seizing new opportunities, and fostering organizational resilience, businesses can thrive and flourish. In the subsequent sections of this chapter, we will explore techniques for fostering a culture of innovation, identifying market trends, developing innovative products or services, and leveraging technology for business growth. These insights will provide you with practical guidance and inspiration to embrace innovation and adaptation in your own business journey.

Section 2: Fostering a Culture of Innovation

In this section, we will delve into the techniques and strategies for fostering a culture of innovation within an organization. Building a culture that encourages creative thinking, embraces change, and values innovation is crucial for driving business growth and staying competitive. Whether you are a business leader, manager, or team member, understanding the importance of fostering a culture of innovation is essential. Let's explore this topic further and discover how you can cultivate a culture that sparks innovation and drives success.

1. **Understanding the Importance of a Culture of Innovation**

    A culture of innovation goes beyond sporadic bursts of creativity; it is a systematic approach that permeates the entire organization. It creates an environment where innovation becomes an integral part of the company's DNA. Such a culture values and promotes forward-thinking, risk-taking, and the pursuit of new ideas and solutions. Fostering a culture of innovation is crucial because it:

    a. **Drives Business Growth:** Innovation is the key driver of growth in today's dynamic business landscape. It helps companies differentiate themselves from competitors, create new products or services, enter new markets, and respond to changing customer needs.

b. **Enhances Employee Engagement:** A culture of innovation empowers employees, making them feel valued and engaged. It encourages them to contribute their ideas and perspectives, fostering a sense of ownership and commitment to the organization's success.

c. **Attracts and Retains Top Talent:** In today's competitive job market, top talent seeks opportunities to work in organizations that foster innovation. A culture of innovation not only attracts skilled professionals but also retains them by providing an environment that nurtures their creativity and growth.

d. **Increases Agility and Adaptability:** A culture of innovation promotes a mindset that is open to change and adaptation. It enables organizations to respond quickly to market shifts, seize opportunities, and navigate challenges effectively.

2. **Embracing Change and Uncertainty**

Fostering a culture of innovation requires embracing change and uncertainty. It involves challenging existing processes, questioning assumptions, and embracing new ways of doing things. Here are some techniques to promote a culture of embracing change:

a. **Encourage Risk-Taking:** Create an environment where calculated risks are encouraged and failure is seen as a learning opportunity. Encourage employees to step out of their comfort zones and explore innovative ideas and approaches.

b. **Foster a Growth Mindset:** Instill a growth mindset in the organization, where challenges are seen as opportunities for growth and learning. Emphasize that innovation requires experimentation, and failures are part of the process.

c. **Lead by Example:** Leaders play a crucial role in fostering a culture of embracing change. Demonstrate a willingness to embrace new ideas, take risks, and adapt to changing circumstances. Encourage open and transparent communication, where employees feel comfortable expressing their ideas and concerns.

3. **Promoting Creative Thinking and Idea Generation**

To foster a culture of innovation, it is essential to promote and support creative thinking and idea generation. Here are some techniques to encourage creative thinking and idea generation:

a. **Provide Time and Space for Creativity:** Dedicate specific time for employees to focus on brainstorming, ideation sessions, and creative problem-solving. Create physical or virtual spaces where employees can collaborate and exchange ideas freely.

b. **Encourage Cross-Functional Collaboration:** Foster collaboration among individuals from different departments or disciplines. Encourage them to share their expertise, collaborate on projects, and exchange ideas. This diversity of perspectives can lead to innovative solutions and breakthrough ideas.

c. c. Provide Resources and Tools: Ensure that employees have access to the necessary resources, such as training, workshops, innovation labs, and technology tools, to support their creative endeavors. Empower them with the tools they need to bring their ideas to life.

4. **Empowering and Supporting Employees**

Empowering and supporting employees is crucial for fostering a culture of innovation. Here are some techniques to empower and support employees:

   a. **Provide Autonomy and Decision-Making Authority**: Give employees the autonomy to explore their ideas, make decisions, and take ownership of their projects. Empower them to experiment and innovate within their areas of expertise.

   b. **Offer Training and Development Opportunities:** Provide training programs and development opportunities to enhance employees' skills and knowledge. This can include innovation workshops, design thinking training, or courses on emerging technologies.

   c. **Establish Feedback Channels:** Create regular feedback channels that allow employees to share their ideas, concerns, and suggestions. Actively listen to their feedback, acknowledge their contributions, and provide constructive feedback to support their growth.

5. **Encouraging Collaboration and Knowledge Sharing**

Collaboration and knowledge sharing play a significant role in fostering a culture of innovation. Here are some techniques to encourage collaboration and knowledge sharing:

a. **Foster a Supportive Environment:** Create an environment where collaboration is encouraged, and teamwork is valued. Encourage employees to share their ideas, seek input from others, and collaborate on projects.

b. **Establish Cross-Functional Teams:** Form cross-functional teams that bring together individuals with diverse skills and expertise. Encourage them to collaborate on projects, solve problems collectively, and learn from each other.

c. **Recognize and Celebrate Collaboration:** Recognize and celebrate successful collaboration efforts within the organization. Highlight team achievements, share success stories, and provide opportunities for cross-team recognition and collaboration.

6. **Recognizing and Rewarding Innovation**

Recognizing and rewarding innovation is essential for reinforcing a culture of innovation. Here are some techniques to recognize and reward innovation:

a. **Celebrate Innovation Events:** Organize events or ceremonies to celebrate innovative ideas, projects, and their impact on the organization. This can be in the form of innovation awards, innovation showcases, or innovation fairs.

b. **Incentives and Rewards:** Implement incentive programs that reward employees for their innovative contributions. This can include monetary rewards, bonuses, promotions, or additional benefits.

c. **Career Development Opportunities**: Provide opportunities for employees to grow and advance their careers based on their innovative achievements. This can include offering special projects, leadership roles, or cross-functional opportunities.

d. **Public Recognition:** Publicly recognize and showcase innovative individuals or teams through internal newsletters, company-wide announcements, or social media platforms. This helps create a sense of pride and encourages others to contribute their innovative ideas.

e. **Knowledge Sharing and Learning:** Encourage employees to share their innovation experiences and lessons learned through knowledge-sharing sessions or internal workshops. This promotes learning and inspires others to innovate.

In conclusion, fostering a culture of innovation requires a deliberate and strategic approach. By understanding the importance of a culture of innovation, embracing change, promoting creative thinking, empowering employees, encouraging collaboration, and recognizing innovation, organizations can create an environment that nurtures and drives continuous innovation. The techniques and strategies discussed in this section provide a foundation for cultivating a culture of innovation within your organization. However, it's important to adapt these practices to your specific context and organizational culture. Remember, fostering a culture of innovation is an ongoing journey that requires commitment and continuous improvement. By fostering a culture of innovation, you can position your organization for sustained growth and success in an ever-evolving business landscape.

Section 3: Identifying Market Trends and Anticipating Customer Needs

In this section, we will explore the importance of identifying market trends and anticipating customer needs as key drivers of innovation and business growth. Understanding market trends and staying ahead of customer needs is crucial for developing innovative products or services that meet the changing demands of your target audience. Let's delve into this topic, providing insights and guidance on how to identify market trends, anticipate customer needs, and develop innovative solutions.

1. **Understanding Market Trends**

   Market trends refer to the patterns, shifts, and developments that occur within a specific industry or market. These trends can be influenced by various factors, including technological advancements, economic changes, social and cultural shifts, and emerging customer preferences. Identifying market trends helps businesses stay informed about the evolving landscape in which they operate.

   Here's how you can gain a better understanding of market trends:

   a. **Market Research:** Conduct comprehensive market research to gather data and insights into your industry. This can include analyzing industry reports, competitor analysis, customer surveys, and studying consumer behavior patterns.

   b. **Industry Events and Conferences:** Attend industry events, conferences, and trade shows to stay updated on the latest innovations, emerging technologies, and market developments. Engage with industry experts, thought leaders, and peers to gain valuable insights and network.

c. **Monitoring Industry Publications:** Keep a close eye on industry publications, news sources, blogs, and social media platforms related to your industry. These platforms often provide valuable information about emerging trends, market disruptions, and industry insights.

d. **Engage in Networking:** Build relationships with professionals in your industry through networking events, online communities, and industry forums. Engaging in conversations with industry peers can provide you with valuable insights into market trends and emerging opportunities.

2. **Anticipating Customer Needs**

Anticipating customer needs is essential for developing innovative products or services that cater to the changing demands and preferences of your target audience. By understanding your customers' pain points, motivations, and aspirations, you can stay ahead of the competition and provide solutions that truly resonate.

Here's how you can anticipate customer needs:

a. **Customer Research:** Conduct in-depth customer research to gain a deep understanding of your target audience. This can include surveys, interviews, focus groups, and user testing. Identify their needs, preferences, and challenges to uncover opportunities for innovation.

b. **Analyze Customer Feedback:** Pay attention to customer feedback, reviews, and complaints. Look for patterns and identify areas where your products or services can be improved or new solutions can be developed to address their needs.

c. **Stay Connected:** Establish channels of communication with your customers, such as social media, email newsletters, and customer support. Engage in conversations, listen to their feedback, and respond to their queries. This direct interaction can provide valuable insights into their evolving needs.

d. **Observe Changing Behaviors:** Monitor changes in customer behavior, such as shifting preferences, adoption of new technologies, or emerging lifestyle trends. These behavioral changes can indicate new opportunities for innovation.

3. **Developing Innovative Solutions**

Once you have identified market trends and anticipated customer needs, the next step is to develop innovative solutions that address those needs effectively.

Here's how you can foster innovation and develop groundbreaking products or services:

a. **Cross-Functional Collaboration:** Foster collaboration among different teams and departments within your organization. Encourage diverse perspectives and expertise to contribute to the innovation process. Create cross-functional teams that work together to develop and refine innovative ideas.

b. **Embrace Design Thinking:** Adopt a design thinking approach, which emphasizes understanding customer needs, rapid prototyping, and iterative development. This user-centric approach helps you create solutions that truly meet customer expectations.

c. **Encourage Experimentation:** Create a culture that encourages experimentation and embraces failure as a learning opportunity. Allow employees to test new ideas, explore different approaches, and take calculated risks in the pursuit of innovation.

d. **Leverage Technology:** Embrace technology and digital transformation to drive innovation. Explore emerging technologies that can enhance your products or services, streamline processes, or open new business opportunities.

e. **Continuous Improvement**: Encourage a mindset of continuous improvement and learning. Regularly review and analyze customer feedback, monitor market trends, and refine your offerings to stay relevant and competitive.

In conclusion, identifying market trends and anticipating customer needs are essential components of developing innovative products or services. By staying informed about market trends, understanding your customers' evolving needs, and fostering a culture of innovation, you can drive business growth and stay competitive in a rapidly changing business landscape. The insights and guidance provided in this section serve as a foundation for successfully identifying market trends, anticipating customer needs, and developing innovative solutions. Remember, innovation is an ongoing process that requires a deep understanding of your market, your customers, and a commitment to continuous improvement.

Section 4: Leveraging Technology and Digital Transformation

In this section, we will delve deeper into the role of technology and digital transformation in enabling business growth and driving innovation. We will provide more detailed guidance for readers with little to no knowledge about the topic, offering actionable insights on how to effectively leverage technology and navigate the digital transformation journey.

1. **The Role of Technology in Business Growth**

   Technology plays a critical role in driving business growth by enabling organizations to streamline processes, improve productivity, and enhance customer experiences. Here are some key aspects to consider:

   a. **Operational Efficiency:** Technology can significantly improve operational efficiency by automating manual tasks, streamlining workflows, and optimizing resource allocation. Consider implementing tools such as project management software, inventory management systems, and workflow automation platforms to eliminate bottlenecks, reduce errors, and improve overall productivity.

   b. **Enhanced Customer Experiences:** Technology enables businesses to deliver personalized and seamless customer experiences. Leverage customer data analytics to gain insights into customer preferences, behaviors, and needs. Implement CRM systems to centralize customer information and provide a unified view across various touchpoints. Utilize marketing automation platforms to deliver targeted and personalized messages to customers at different stages of their journey.

c. **Access to New Markets:** The digital landscape offers businesses opportunities to access new markets and expand their customer base. Establish an online presence through a well-designed website, optimize it for search engines, and leverage digital advertising channels to reach and engage with a broader audience. Consider utilizing e-commerce platforms or online marketplaces to extend your reach and sell products or services globally.

d. **Innovation and Differentiation:** Technology serves as a catalyst for innovation, enabling businesses to develop new products, services, and business models. Explore emerging technologies such as AI, IoT, and AR to identify ways they can enhance your offerings. For instance, AI-powered chatbots can provide 24/7 customer support, IoT devices can gather real-time data for improved decision-making, and AR can offer immersive experiences to customers.

2. **Embracing Digital Transformation**

Assess Current State: Conduct a comprehensive assessment of your current digital capabilities, including infrastructure, systems, processes, and skills. Identify areas that require improvement or transformation to align with your business goals and customer expectations.

a. **Define a Digital Strategy:** Develop a clear digital strategy that outlines your objectives, target outcomes, and key initiatives. Align your digital strategy with your overall business strategy and ensure it addresses the evolving needs of your customers. Consider factors such as market trends, competitive landscape, and technological advancements in shaping your strategy.

b. **Technology Integration:** Invest in technology solutions that align with your digital strategy. This may include cloud computing for scalability and flexibility, data analytics tools for insights-driven decision-making, and collaboration platforms for seamless communication. Ensure proper integration of these technologies to create an interconnected and efficient digital ecosystem.

c. **Foster a Digital Culture:** Cultivate a culture of digital innovation within your organization. Encourage employees to embrace technology, adapt to change, and continuously upskill. Establish channels for sharing ideas and fostering collaboration across teams. Encourage experimentation, risk-taking, and learning from failures as valuable opportunities for growth.

d. **Customer-Centric Approach:** Place the customer at the center of your digital transformation efforts. Use data analytics to understand customer behavior, preferences, and pain points. Leverage technology to deliver personalized experiences, anticipate customer needs, and provide proactive support. Continuously seek feedback and engage customers in co-creation to drive innovation.

e. **Data-Driven Decision Making:** Develop a data-driven mindset within your organization. Collect and analyze data from various sources to gain insights into market trends, customer behavior, and operational performance. Utilize data visualization tools and dashboards to monitor key metrics and make informed decisions. Leverage predictive analytics to anticipate market shifts and customer needs.

f. **Agile and Iterative Approach:** Embrace an agile and iterative approach to digital transformation. Break down transformation initiatives into smaller, manageable projects or sprints. Continuously gather feedback, learn from outcomes, and iterate on your strategies. Embrace an organizational structure that supports agility, collaboration, and cross-functional teams.

By effectively leveraging technology and embracing digital transformation, businesses can unlock new growth opportunities, improve operational efficiency, and stay competitive in a rapidly evolving digital landscape. The detailed guidance provided in this section serves as a roadmap for embracing technology and driving digital transformation within your organization. Remember, digital transformation is a journey that requires commitment, continuous learning, and a customer-centric mindset. Embrace the power of technology to innovate, adapt, and thrive in the digital era.

Here is a real-life example of innovation and adaptation's importance:

3M is a prime example of a company that has consistently embraced innovation and adaptation to drive sustainable growth. Founded in 1902 as the Minnesota Mining and Manufacturing Company, 3M has evolved into a global powerhouse known for its innovative products and solutions.

At the heart of 3M's success is its commitment to fostering a culture of innovation. The company encourages its employees to pursue creative thinking, take risks, and explore new ideas. This culture of innovation is exemplified by 3M's famous "15% time" policy, where employees are given the freedom to dedicate a portion of their work hours to pursue their own projects and ideas.

One of 3M's most iconic innovations is the Post-it Note, which revolutionized the way we communicate and organize information. Initially, the invention of the Post-it Note was considered a failure as it was a result of a failed attempt to create a strong adhesive. However, rather than discarding the idea, 3M recognized its potential and turned it into a successful product that has become a staple in offices and households worldwide.

Beyond Post-it Notes, 3M has continuously expanded its product portfolio through groundbreaking research and development. The company operates in diverse industries, ranging from healthcare and transportation to consumer goods and electronics. Their innovative products include everything from Scotch tape and respirators to reflective materials and advanced adhesives.

3M's commitment to innovation is further reflected in its strategic acquisitions and partnerships. The company actively seeks collaborations with external innovators, startups, and research institutions to leverage new technologies and ideas. This approach enables 3M to stay at the forefront of industry trends and access expertise beyond its internal capabilities.

Moreover, 3M's ability to anticipate customer needs and adapt to changing market demands has been a key driver of its sustained growth. The company invests heavily in market research and customer insights, allowing them to understand emerging trends and identify unmet needs. This customer-centric approach has enabled 3M to develop innovative solutions that address real-world challenges and provide value to their customers.

Throughout its history, 3M has demonstrated resilience and agility in adapting to market shifts. The company continually evolves its product offerings and diversifies its business to stay relevant. By embracing digital transformation and leveraging technology, 3M has found new ways to connect with customers, streamline operations, and drive efficiency.

The story of 3M serves as an inspiration for businesses seeking sustainable growth through innovation and adaptation. It showcases the power of fostering a culture of innovation, embracing failure as an opportunity for learning, and staying customer-focused in an ever-changing marketplace. By embracing the spirit of 3M, businesses can unleash their own potential for innovation and adaptation, setting themselves up for long-term success in a dynamic business landscape.

How can your business be like 3M?

Conclusion

Innovation and adaptation are crucial elements for driving business growth and staying competitive in today's rapidly evolving market landscape. Throughout this chapter, we have explored the significance of innovation and adaptation as key drivers of success. We discussed techniques for fostering a culture of innovation, encouraging creative thinking, and embracing change within organizations. By creating an environment that nurtures innovation, businesses can unlock their full potential and position themselves for sustainable growth.

We also delved into the importance of identifying market trends and anticipating customer needs. By closely monitoring market dynamics, businesses can stay ahead of the curve and proactively respond to emerging opportunities. Understanding customer preferences, pain points, and expectations enables organizations to develop innovative products or services that address those needs effectively.

Furthermore, we explored the role of technology and digital transformation in enabling business growth and innovation. Embracing technological advancements and leveraging digital tools can revolutionize the way businesses operate, connect with customers, and optimize their processes. From implementing automation and data analytics to adopting cloud computing and artificial intelligence, technology offers immense potential for driving innovation and achieving sustainable growth.

To illustrate the power of innovation and adaptation, we shared the inspiring story of 3M, a company that has consistently embraced innovation throughout its history. By fostering a culture of creativity, empowering employees to explore new ideas, and encouraging risk-taking, 3M has revolutionized multiple industries and sustained long-term growth.

As we conclude this chapter, it is important to recognize that innovation and adaptation are ongoing processes. Businesses must continuously seek opportunities for improvement, challenge the status quo, and adapt to the ever-changing market landscape. By embracing a mindset of continuous learning and improvement, organizations can navigate challenges, seize new opportunities, and position themselves for long-term success.

In the next chapter, we will delve into the exciting world of customer experience and its impact on business growth. We will explore strategies for delivering exceptional customer experiences, building lasting relationships, and driving customer loyalty. By prioritizing customer-centricity and delivering memorable experiences, businesses can differentiate themselves in the market and foster sustainable growth.

So, get ready to embark on a journey into the realm of customer experience and discover how it can transform your business. Stay tuned for valuable insights, practical tips, and real-life examples that will empower you to elevate your customer experience and drive growth.

Part 4: Navigating Financial Challenges

Chapter 7: Managing Finances for Growth

---◦◇◦---

Introduction

Managing finances effectively is a critical aspect of business growth and expansion. In this chapter, we will delve into the financial considerations and challenges that businesses face during periods of growth. We will explore strategies for managing cash flow, securing funding, and optimizing financial resources. Additionally, we will provide guidance on financial planning, budgeting, and forecasting to ensure sustainable growth. By understanding the role of financial metrics and key performance indicators (KPIs), businesses can monitor their performance and make informed decisions. Throughout the chapter, we will also highlight case studies and examples of businesses that effectively managed their finances during growth phases.

Section 1: Financial Considerations and Challenges of Business Growth

When embarking on a journey of business growth and expansion, it is essential to understand the financial considerations and challenges that come with it. While growth brings exciting opportunities, it also poses unique financial complexities that require careful management. In this section, we will delve deeper into the various financial considerations and challenges associated with business growth, providing you with a comprehensive understanding and actionable guidance to navigate them effectively.

1. **Financial Planning and Goal Setting**

   Financial planning is the foundation of successful business growth. It involves setting clear financial goals and developing strategies to achieve them. During the growth phase, it is crucial to reassess your financial plan and align it with your expansion objectives. This includes projecting revenue growth, estimating expenses, and allocating resources accordingly. By having a well-defined financial plan, you can make informed decisions, allocate resources effectively, and track your progress towards your growth goals.

2. **Funding for Growth**

   One of the primary challenges in business growth is securing the necessary funding. As you expand your operations, you may require additional capital to invest in new equipment, hire more employees, develop new products or services, or enter new markets. It is important to assess your funding needs and explore various sources of capital, such as bank loans, lines of credit, equity financing, or government grants. Each funding option has its own requirements, terms, and implications, so it is crucial to carefully evaluate and select the most suitable option for your business.

3. **Cash Flow Management**

   Managing cash flow becomes increasingly important during periods of growth. As your business expands, you may experience fluctuations in cash inflows and outflows. It is crucial to have a clear understanding of your cash flow dynamics, ensuring that you have enough liquidity to cover operational expenses, meet financial obligations, and fund growth initiatives. Implementing effective cash flow management practices, such as optimizing accounts receivable and payable, maintaining an adequate cash reserve, and managing inventory levels, will help you navigate cash flow challenges and maintain a healthy financial position.

4. **Cost Control and Efficiency**

Business growth often comes with increased expenses, making cost control and efficiency paramount. As you scale your operations, it is important to carefully monitor and manage your expenses. This includes analyzing your cost structure, identifying areas for optimization, and implementing strategies to improve efficiency. Negotiating favorable terms with suppliers, implementing cost-saving measures, and leveraging technology to automate processes can help you streamline operations and reduce unnecessary expenditures, ultimately improving profitability and supporting sustainable growth.

5. **Financial Risk Management**

As your business expands, it is essential to assess and manage financial risks effectively. Growth brings inherent risks, such as market volatility, economic fluctuations, or changes in customer preferences. Conducting a comprehensive risk assessment and developing risk management strategies will help you mitigate potential threats to your financial stability. This may involve diversifying your revenue streams, implementing risk management policies, and maintaining adequate insurance coverage. Being prepared for unexpected financial challenges will strengthen your resilience and ensure the continuity of your growth trajectory.

6. Monitoring and Performance Measurement

To drive successful growth, it is crucial to monitor and measure your financial performance regularly. Key financial metrics and key performance indicators (KPIs) can provide valuable insights into the health and progress of your business. By tracking metrics such as revenue growth, profitability, return on investment, and cash flow ratios, you can evaluate the effectiveness of your growth strategies, identify areas for improvement, and make data-driven decisions. Regular financial reporting and analysis enable you to stay proactive and adjust your strategies as needed.

By understanding and effectively managing these financial considerations and challenges, you can navigate the complexities of business growth and position your company for sustainable success. Engaging in sound financial planning, exploring funding options, implementing robust cash flow management practices, controlling costs, mitigating financial risks, and monitoring performance are all crucial components of managing finances for growth. Seeking the guidance of financial professionals, such as accountants or financial advisors, can also provide valuable insights and expertise to support your financial management efforts.

In the next sections of this chapter, we will delve deeper into specific strategies for managing cash flow, securing funding, financial planning, and monitoring business performance. Through practical guidance and real-life examples, you will gain actionable insights to effectively manage your finances and drive sustainable growth.

Section 2: Managing Cash Flow for Growth

Cash flow management is a critical aspect of managing finances for business growth. It involves maintaining a healthy balance between cash inflows and outflows to ensure the smooth operation of your business. Without proper cash flow management, even a profitable business can face challenges in meeting its financial obligations, funding growth initiatives, and seizing opportunities. In this section, we will explore effective strategies for managing cash flow, securing funding, and optimizing financial resources, providing you with valuable insights and actionable guidance to support your growth initiatives.

1. **Cash Flow Forecasting:**

   Cash flow forecasting is an essential tool for managing cash flow during periods of growth. It involves projecting your expected cash inflows and outflows over a specific period, typically on a monthly or quarterly basis. By forecasting your cash flow, you can anticipate potential cash shortages or surpluses and take proactive measures to address them. This allows you to make informed decisions about managing expenses, timing investments, and negotiating payment terms with suppliers or customers. Regularly reviewing and updating your cash flow forecast will help you maintain a clear picture of your financial position and make timely adjustments as needed.

   Guidance:

   To effectively manage your cash flow, start by gathering historical financial data and analyzing trends. Identify the key drivers of your cash inflows and outflows, such as sales revenue, accounts receivable, inventory levels, operating expenses, and accounts payable. Utilize financial software or tools to create a cash flow forecast that incorporates these factors and provides you with a comprehensive view of your cash position. Continuously monitor your actual cash flow against your forecast and adjust your operations or financial strategy as necessary.

2. **Efficient Accounts Receivable Management**

Optimizing your accounts receivable process is crucial for maintaining a healthy cash flow. Late or delayed payments from customers can strain your cash flow, especially during periods of growth when expenses may be higher. Implementing strategies to improve the collection of outstanding invoices can help you accelerate cash inflows. This includes establishing clear payment terms, sending timely and accurate invoices, and following up with customers on overdue payments. Offering incentives for early payment, such as discounts or rewards, or implementing automated payment systems can also expedite the receipt of funds. Regularly monitoring and managing your accounts receivable will help you minimize outstanding balances and improve your cash flow position.

Guidance:

To effectively manage accounts receivable, establish a streamlined invoicing process that ensures prompt and accurate billing. Clearly communicate your payment terms to customers and provide multiple payment options to facilitate timely payments. Implement a system for tracking and following up on overdue payments, and consider using automated reminders or collection agencies when necessary. Regularly review your accounts receivable aging report to identify any bottlenecks or patterns of late payment. By proactively managing your accounts receivable, you can enhance cash flow and reduce the risk of bad debts.

3. **Effective Accounts Payable Management**

Managing your accounts payable is equally important for cash flow management. By carefully managing your payment obligations, you can optimize your cash outflows. This includes negotiating favorable payment terms with suppliers, taking advantage of early payment discounts, and optimizing your payment schedule to align with your cash flow. Additionally, reviewing and analyzing your expenses regularly can help identify areas where cost savings can be achieved. Efficient accounts payable management will ensure that you maintain strong relationships with your suppliers while saving cash for other growth-related expenses.

Guidance:

Establish clear processes for managing accounts payable, including setting up vendor accounts, documenting purchase orders and receipts, and tracking payment due dates. Regularly review your vendor contracts to identify opportunities for negotiation, such as extended payment terms or volume discounts. Take advantage of early payment discounts offered by suppliers, but balance this with your cash flow needs. Implement a robust system for monitoring and tracking your accounts payable to avoid late payments or penalties. By optimizing your accounts payable, you can maintain positive relationships with suppliers while effectively managing your cash flow.

4. **Working Capital Optimization**

Working capital refers to the funds available for day-to-day operations. Optimizing your working capital is crucial for managing cash flow during growth phases. This involves carefully managing your inventory levels, ensuring that they align with customer demand and sales forecasts. Excessive inventory ties up valuable cash, while inadequate inventory can lead to missed sales opportunities. Additionally, effectively managing your accounts receivable and accounts payable, as discussed earlier, contributes to optimizing working capital. By striking the right balance between these elements, you can enhance cash flow and support your growth initiatives.

Guidance:

Conduct a thorough analysis of your inventory management processes, including demand forecasting, order quantities, and lead times. Implement inventory management techniques such as just-in-time (JIT) or lean inventory practices to minimize holding costs and reduce the risk of obsolete inventory. Regularly review your sales forecasts and adjust your inventory levels accordingly. Explore opportunities to collaborate with suppliers to manage inventory more efficiently, such as implementing vendor-managed inventory (VMI) programs. By optimizing your working capital, you can free up cash for investment in growth opportunities and ensure the smooth operation of your business.

5. Securing Funding for Growth

Funding is often required to fuel business growth and expansion. Exploring different funding options is crucial for managing cash flow effectively. This may involve obtaining loans from financial institutions, seeking venture capital or private equity investments, or considering crowdfunding platforms. Each funding option has its own requirements and implications, so it is essential to thoroughly evaluate and select the most suitable option for your business. Additionally, maintaining a strong relationship with your financial partners and proactively communicating your growth plans and financial projections can help secure the necessary funding to support your expansion.

Guidance:

Start by assessing your funding needs and determining the amount of capital required to support your growth plans. Research various funding options and carefully evaluate their terms, interest rates, repayment terms, and potential impact on your cash flow. Prepare a comprehensive business plan and financial projections to present to potential lenders or investors. Build relationships with financial institutions or investors who specialize in funding businesses in your industry or growth stage. Regularly review your financial performance and update your projections to demonstrate your ability to generate returns on investment. By strategically securing funding, you can access the necessary capital to support your growth initiatives and manage cash flow effectively.

6. Optimal Resource Allocation

As your business grows, it is crucial to optimize the allocation of your financial resources. This includes aligning your budget with your growth goals and prioritizing investments that yield the highest return on investment (ROI). Conducting a cost-benefit analysis of potential growth initiatives will help you make informed decisions about resource allocation. Additionally, monitoring the financial performance of different business segments or projects will enable you to identify areas where resources can be reallocated to drive greater growth and profitability.

Guidance:

> Start by creating a comprehensive budget that aligns with your growth plans and financial projections. Identify the key areas where investments are required to support your growth, such as marketing, research and development, talent acquisition, or infrastructure. Prioritize these investments based on their potential impact on revenue growth, customer acquisition, or operational efficiency. Regularly review your financial performance against your budget and adjust as needed. Continuously monitor the return on investment for different projects or initiatives and reallocate resources to maximize growth opportunities.

By implementing these strategies for managing cash flow, securing funding, and optimizing financial resources, you can effectively navigate the financial challenges of business growth. Regularly monitoring your cash flow, actively managing accounts receivable and accounts payable, optimizing working capital, securing the right funding, and allocating resources strategically will ensure the financial health and sustainability of your business as you pursue growth.

In the next sections of this chapter, we will delve deeper into financial planning, budgeting, forecasting, and monitoring business performance. By gaining a comprehensive understanding of these concepts and implementing sound financial practices, you will be well-equipped to manage your finances effectively and drive sustainable growth for your business. Remember, cash flow management is a continuous process that requires regular monitoring, evaluation, and adjustment. Stay proactive in your financial management practices to ensure the long-term success of your business.

Section 3: Financial Planning and Budgeting for Sustainable Growth

Financial planning and budgeting play a crucial role in driving sustainable growth for your business. They provide a strategic framework for managing your finances, allocating resources, and making informed decisions that support your growth objectives. Here's a more comprehensive breakdown of the guidance on financial planning, budgeting, and forecasting for sustainable growth:

1. Financial Planning:

    a. **Set Clear Goals:** Setting clear financial goals is essential for guiding your business's growth trajectory. By defining long-term and short-term goals, you provide a clear direction for your financial planning efforts. These goals serve as benchmarks for measuring your progress and help align your financial decisions with your business objectives.

    b. **Assess Business Risks:** Evaluating and managing risks is an integral part of financial planning. By identifying potential risks, such as market fluctuations, regulatory changes, or competitive pressures, you can develop strategies to mitigate their impact. This proactive approach helps safeguard your financial stability and supports sustainable growth.

c. **Analyze Market Trends:** Keeping a pulse on market trends is crucial for effective financial planning. Understanding market dynamics, industry developments, and customer preferences enables you to adapt your strategies and allocate resources appropriately. By aligning your financial plans with market trends, you can seize opportunities and stay ahead of the competition.

2. **Budgeting:**

   a. **Revenue Forecasting:** Accurate revenue forecasting provides a foundation for sound financial planning. By analyzing historical data, market research, and sales projections, you can estimate future revenue streams. This insight enables you to make informed decisions about resource allocation, investment opportunities, and growth strategies.

   b. **Expense Management:** Effective expense management is vital for optimizing your financial resources. By categorizing expenses, analyzing cost structures, and prioritizing expenditures, you can identify areas for cost reduction and efficiency improvement. This disciplined approach ensures that your financial resources are directed towards activities that generate the greatest return on investment.

   c. **Capital Expenditure Planning:** Thoughtful capital expenditure planning supports sustainable growth by allocating resources to strategic investments. By evaluating capital expenditure needs, assessing ROI, and prioritizing investments, you can enhance operational efficiency, expand your capabilities, and position your business for long-term success.

3. **Cash Flow Projection:**

   a. **Cash Flow Forecast:** Cash flow projection is essential for maintaining healthy liquidity and managing day-to-day operations. By estimating the timing and amount of cash inflows and outflows, you can identify potential cash flow gaps or surpluses. This knowledge enables you to make informed decisions regarding working capital management, financing options, and growth initiatives.

   b. **Working Capital Management:** Efficient working capital management is critical for maintaining a balanced financial position. By optimizing inventory levels, managing receivables and payables, and reducing cash conversion cycles, you can improve cash flow, minimize liquidity risks, and support sustainable growth.

4. **Monitoring and Analysis:**

   a. **Financial Reporting:** Timely and accurate financial reporting provides a comprehensive view of your business's financial health. By generating regular financial statements, you gain insights into revenue, expenses, assets, liabilities, and cash flow. This information allows you to assess performance, identify trends, and make data-driven decisions to drive growth.

   b. **Performance Measurement:** Key performance indicators (KPIs) are essential tools for measuring your financial performance and progress towards your growth goals. By monitoring KPIs such as revenue growth rate, gross profit margin, ROI, and working capital ratio, you can track your performance, identify areas for improvement, and make strategic adjustments to your financial plans.

5. **Seek Professional Advice:**

   a. Engaging with financial professionals, such as accountants, financial advisors, or consultants, can provide invaluable support in financial planning and budgeting. Their expertise and experience can help you interpret financial data, navigate complex regulations, and optimize your financial strategies. Consider seeking professional advice to ensure your financial plans align with industry best practices and maximize growth potential.

By incorporating these practices into your financial planning and budgeting processes, you can effectively manage your finances, optimize resource allocation, and position your business for sustainable growth. Regular monitoring, analysis, and adjustments are key to adapting to changing business conditions, market dynamics, and growth objectives. Remember, financial planning and budgeting are ongoing processes that require a proactive and strategic approach to support your business's long-term success.

Section 4: Monitoring Performance with Financial Metrics and KPIs

Monitoring business performance is essential for assessing the effectiveness of your financial strategies and ensuring sustainable growth. Financial metrics and key performance indicators (KPIs) provide valuable insights into your business's financial health, efficiency, and profitability. Here's a more comprehensive explanation of the role of financial metrics and KPIs in monitoring business performance:

1. **Understanding Financial Metrics**

   Financial metrics are quantitative measures that assess various aspects of your business's financial performance. They provide objective data that reflects your business's profitability, liquidity, efficiency, and stability. Here are some key financial metrics:

   a. **Revenue:** Revenue represents the total income generated from sales of products or services. Tracking revenue helps evaluate the effectiveness of your sales and marketing efforts and assess overall business growth.

   b. **Gross Profit Margin:** Gross profit margin measures the profitability of your core operations by calculating the percentage of revenue remaining after deducting the cost of goods sold. It reflects your business's ability to generate profits from its products or services.

   c. **Net Profit Margin:** Net profit margin assesses your business's overall profitability by calculating the percentage of revenue remaining after deducting all expenses, including operating costs, taxes, and interest. It reflects the efficiency of your cost management and pricing strategies.

   d. **Return on Investment (ROI):** ROI measures the return on investment generated from a particular project or initiative. It compares the gains or benefits achieved relative to the cost of investment, providing insights into the profitability and efficiency of your investments.

   e. **Cash Flow:** Cash flow represents the movement of cash in and out of your business over a specific period. Monitoring cash flow helps ensure sufficient liquidity for operational needs and identifies potential cash flow challenges.

2. **Key Performance Indicators (KPIs)**

KPIs are specific metrics that reflect the performance of critical areas within your business. They help you assess progress toward your strategic objectives and highlight areas requiring improvement. Here are some key financial KPIs:

   a. **Revenue Growth Rate:** Revenue growth rate measures the percentage increase or decrease in revenue over a specific period. It indicates the success of your sales and marketing strategies and provides insights into your business's expansion.

   b. **Gross Margin:** Gross margin assesses the profitability of each unit of product or service sold by calculating the difference between the selling price and the direct costs of production or provision. Monitoring gross margin helps identify pricing and cost efficiency opportunities.

   c. **Debt-to-Equity Ratio:** The debt-to-equity ratio compares the total debt of your business to its total equity. It reflects the proportion of debt financing relative to equity financing and indicates the level of financial risk and leverage in your business.

   d. **Current Ratio:** The current ratio measures your business's liquidity and ability to meet short-term obligations. It compares current assets (e.g., cash, inventory, accounts receivable) to current liabilities (e.g., accounts payable, short-term loans), providing insights into your financial stability.

e. **Operating Cash Flow Ratio:** The operating cash flow ratio assesses your business's ability to generate sufficient cash flow from its operations to cover operational expenses and investment needs. It reflects the efficiency and sustainability of your cash flow.

3. **Role of Financial Metrics and KPIs**

Financial metrics and KPIs serve several important purposes in monitoring business performance:

a. **Performance Evaluation:** Financial metrics and KPIs allow you to objectively assess your business's financial performance, identify strengths and weaknesses, and track progress toward your goals. They provide a clear picture of how well your business is performing financially.

b. **Decision Making:** By monitoring financial metrics and KPIs, you can make informed decisions regarding resource allocation, investment opportunities, pricing strategies, cost management, and growth initiatives. They provide the necessary data to guide your financial decision-making process.

c. **Benchmarking:** Financial metrics and KPIs enable you to compare your business's performance against industry benchmarks or competitors. This benchmarking helps you understand your relative position, identify areas for improvement, and set realistic performance targets.

d. **Early Warning Signs:** Financial metrics and KPIs can act as early warning signs for potential financial issues or risks. By closely monitoring these indicators, you can identify trends, deviations from expected performance, and take timely corrective actions.

e. **Goal Alignment:** Financial metrics and KPIs help align your financial performance with your strategic objectives. They provide a quantifiable way to measure progress toward your goals and ensure that your financial strategies support your overall business strategy.

By regularly monitoring and analyzing financial metrics and KPIs, you can gain valuable insights into your business's financial performance, make informed decisions, and drive sustainable growth. Remember to select metrics and KPIs that align with your specific business goals and industry characteristics. Additionally, establish a consistent tracking and reporting system to ensure accurate and up-to-date information.

Conclusion

In this chapter, we delved into the critical aspects of managing finances for business growth. We discussed the financial considerations and challenges that come with expansion, provided strategies for effectively managing cash flow, securing funding, and optimizing financial resources, and explored the importance of financial planning, budgeting, and forecasting for sustainable growth. Additionally, we highlighted the role of financial metrics and key performance indicators (KPIs) in monitoring business performance.

Managing finances is an essential component of driving business growth and ensuring long-term success. By understanding the financial landscape and challenges that accompany growth, you can make informed decisions and implement effective strategies. The guidance provided in this chapter serves as a valuable resource to navigate financial aspects such as cash flow management, funding, resource optimization, and financial planning.

Effective cash flow management is crucial for sustaining operations, meeting financial obligations, and fueling growth. By employing strategies such as monitoring cash flow, optimizing receivables and payables, and leveraging financing options, you can maintain a healthy cash flow position and seize growth opportunities.

Securing funding is often necessary to support business expansion. We discussed various funding options, including traditional loans, equity financing, grants, and alternative sources. By exploring these options, conducting thorough research, and preparing a compelling funding proposal, you can increase your chances of securing the necessary capital for growth.

Optimizing financial resources involves maximizing the value derived from every dollar spent. Through effective cost management, efficient resource allocation, and leveraging technology, you can streamline operations, improve productivity, and enhance profitability, ultimately driving business growth.

Financial planning, budgeting, and forecasting are critical components of sustainable growth. By developing a comprehensive financial plan, setting realistic budgets, and regularly monitoring and adjusting your financial forecasts, you can align your financial strategies with your business goals, anticipate challenges, and make informed financial decisions.

Furthermore, the use of financial metrics and KPIs allows you to measure and track your business's financial performance. By monitoring metrics such as revenue growth, profitability ratios, liquidity ratios, and return on investment, you can gain valuable insights into your financial health, identify areas for improvement, and make data-driven decisions to drive growth.

In conclusion, effective financial management is vital for driving business growth and ensuring long-term success. By implementing the strategies and practices outlined in this chapter, you can navigate financial challenges, optimize resources, and position your business for sustainable growth.

In the next chapter, we will shift our focus to the importance of leadership and team development in driving business growth. We will explore effective leadership strategies, team-building techniques, and talent development practices that empower your organization to thrive in a dynamic and competitive landscape. Stay tuned for Chapter 8: Leadership and Team Development.

Part 5: Building Strong Leadership and Teams

Chapter 8: Leadership and Team Development

---∘◇∘---

Introduction

In Chapter 8, we will explore the crucial role of strong leadership and effective team development in driving business growth. We will discuss the significance of these factors and how they contribute to creating a thriving and successful organization. This chapter will provide insights, techniques, and guidance on developing leadership skills, fostering a positive work culture, building high-performing teams, recruiting top talent, nurturing employee growth, promoting collaboration and innovation, and creating a culture of accountability.

Section 1: The Importance of Strong Leadership and Effective Team Development

In today's competitive business landscape, strong leadership and effective team development play a pivotal role in driving business growth and success. These factors are essential for creating a cohesive and high-performing organization that can navigate challenges, seize opportunities, and achieve sustainable growth. In this section, we will explore the significance of strong leadership and effective team development, providing context and guidance for readers who may be unfamiliar with these concepts.

1.   The Role of Leadership in Business Growth

Strong leadership is the cornerstone of a thriving organization. Leaders provide vision, direction, and guidance to their teams, inspiring them to work towards common goals. Effective leaders possess a range of qualities, including strategic thinking, strong decision-making abilities, and the capacity to inspire and motivate others. They create a positive work environment that fosters creativity, collaboration, and innovation. Moreover, leaders set the tone for the organizational culture, establishing values and behaviors that drive business growth.

2. **The Benefits of Effective Team Development**

Building and developing high-performing teams is crucial for driving business growth. Effective team development ensures that individuals with complementary skills and expertise come together to work towards shared objectives. When teams are well-developed, they demonstrate enhanced communication, collaboration, and problem-solving abilities. They are more adaptable to change and can leverage the diverse perspectives and talents of team members. This ultimately leads to increased productivity, higher levels of innovation, and improved business outcomes.

3. **Driving Business Growth through Leadership and Team Development**

Strong leadership and effective team development contribute to business growth in several ways:

   a. **Alignment and Goal Achievement:** Strong leaders align the efforts of individuals and teams with the organization's strategic objectives. They ensure that everyone is working towards a common purpose, fostering unity and a sense of purpose among team members. This alignment enables the organization to achieve its goals more efficiently and effectively.

b. **Employee Engagement and Retention:** Effective leadership and team development create an environment where employees feel valued, engaged, and motivated. When employees are engaged, they are more likely to go above and beyond in their roles, leading to increased productivity and performance. Additionally, organizations that invest in developing their employees demonstrate a commitment to their growth, which fosters employee loyalty and retention.

c. **Innovation and Adaptability:** Strong leaders and well-developed teams are essential for fostering a culture of innovation and adaptability. They encourage creative thinking, collaboration, and risk-taking, which are key drivers of innovation. Effective teams are also more adaptable to changes in the business environment, allowing the organization to respond quickly to market shifts and seize new opportunities.

d. **Organizational Resilience:** In the face of challenges and uncertainties, strong leadership and effective team development contribute to organizational resilience. Leaders inspire confidence, provide guidance during turbulent times, and empower teams to overcome obstacles. Well-developed teams are better equipped to handle adversity, adapt to change, and find solutions to complex problems, ensuring the organization's ability to weather challenges and sustain growth.

Guidance:

To drive business growth through strong leadership and effective team development, consider the following guidance:

1. **Invest in Leadership Development:** Develop your leadership skills by seeking opportunities for learning and growth. Enhance your strategic thinking, decision-making, and communication abilities. Foster emotional intelligence and build strong relationships with your team members.

2. **Nurture a Positive Work Culture:** Create a work environment that fosters trust, respect, and open communication. Encourage collaboration, idea-sharing, and feedback. Recognize and reward achievements, and promote work-life balance to enhance employee engagement and satisfaction.

3. **Develop High-Performing Teams:** Build teams with diverse skills and perspectives that complement each other. Establish clear goals, roles, and expectations. Encourage team members to collaborate, share knowledge, and support each other. Provide opportunities for team-building activities and foster a culture of continuous learning.

4. **Empower and Delegate:** Delegate responsibilities to team members, empowering them to make decisions and take ownership of their work. Encourage autonomy and provide support when needed. Foster a culture of accountability, where team members take responsibility for their actions and outcomes.

5. **Foster Innovation and Adaptability:** Encourage creative thinking, risk-taking, and experimentation within your teams. Create platforms for idea-sharing and collaboration. Embrace change and help your team members develop a growth mindset that embraces new challenges and opportunities.

In the next section, we will delve into techniques for developing leadership skills, fostering a positive work culture, and building high-performing teams.

Section 2: Developing Leadership Skills

Effective leadership is a vital component of driving business growth and building high-performing teams. In this section, we will explore various techniques for developing leadership skills, fostering a positive work culture, and cultivating high-performing teams. Whether you are an aspiring leader or already in a leadership role, these strategies will help you enhance your leadership abilities and create an environment where your team can thrive.

1. **Developing Self-Awareness**

   Self-awareness is the foundation of effective leadership. It Involves understanding your strengths, weaknesses, values, and beliefs. By gaining clarity about yourself, you can lead with authenticity and integrity. Self-awareness also enables you to recognize and manage your emotions, enhancing your ability to communicate and connect with others. Techniques for developing self-awareness include:

   a. **Reflective Practices:** Take time for self-reflection, journaling, or meditation to gain insights into your thoughts, feelings, and behaviors.

b. **Seek Feedback:** Actively seek feedback from colleagues, mentors, or coaches to gain an outside perspective on your leadership style.

c. **Personality Assessments:** Utilize tools like personality assessments (e.g., Myers-Briggs Type Indicator) to gain deeper insights into your personality traits and preferences.

2. **Enhancing Communication and Emotional Intelligence**

Effective leaders are skilled communicators who can convey their vision, ideas, and expectations clearly. They also possess high emotional intelligence, which involves understanding and managing their own emotions and empathizing with others. Techniques for enhancing communication and emotional intelligence include:

a. **Active Listening:** Practice active listening by giving your full attention to others, asking clarifying questions, and demonstrating empathy.

b. **Clear and Concise Communication:** Use clear and concise language, avoid jargon, and adapt your communication style to suit different audiences.

c. **Emotional Regulation:** Develop techniques to manage your emotions in challenging situations, such as deep breathing exercises or taking a short break to regain composure.

d. **Empathy:** Put yourself in others' shoes and strive to understand their perspectives, needs, and concerns.

3. **Building a Positive Work Culture**

Creating a positive work culture is essential for attracting and retaining top talent, fostering collaboration, and driving business growth. Techniques for building a positive work culture include:

a. **Define and Communicate Core Values:** Clearly define the core values that guide your organization and ensure they are communicated effectively to all employees.

b. **Lead by Example:** Demonstrate the behaviors and values you expect from your team members. Be approachable, respectful, and supportive.

c. **Encourage Collaboration and Teamwork:** Foster a collaborative environment where team members feel comfortable sharing ideas, collaborating on projects, and supporting each other's growth.

d. **Recognize and Celebrate Achievements:** Regularly acknowledge and celebrate individual and team achievements to boost morale and reinforce a positive work culture.

4. Developing High-Performing Teams

Building high-performing teams is crucial for achieving business growth and success. Techniques for developing high-performing teams include:

a. **Set Clear Goals and Expectations:** Clearly define team goals, roles, and expectations to ensure alignment and accountability.

b. **Foster Trust and Psychological Safety:** Create an environment where team members feel safe to take risks, share ideas, and provide constructive feedback without fear of judgment or reprisal.

c. **Encourage Continuous Learning:** Provide opportunities for professional development, training, and mentorship to support the growth and skill enhancement of team members.

d. **Promote Collaboration and Cross-functional Communication**: Encourage collaboration between team members and foster communication across different departments or functions to drive innovation and problem-solving.

Guidance:

To develop your leadership skills and foster a positive work culture, consider the following guidance:

1. **Invest in Personal Development:** Engage in continuous learning and seek opportunities to enhance your leadership skills through workshops, courses, books, or coaching.

2. **Seek Feedback and Learn from Mistakes:** Actively seek feedback from your team members, peers, and superiors. Embrace constructive criticism and learn from your mistakes to grow as a leader.

3. **Build Relationships:** Cultivate meaningful relationships with your team members based on trust, respect, and open communication. Get to know them on a personal level and show genuine interest in their professional growth.

4. **Lead with Purpose:** Clearly articulate the organization's mission and vision to inspire and motivate your team. Connect their work to a larger purpose and show how it contributes to the organization's success.

5. **Empower and Delegate:** Delegate responsibilities and empower your team members to make decisions and take ownership of their work. Provide guidance and support while allowing them the autonomy to excel.

In the next section, we will delve into guidance on recruiting top talent, nurturing employee growth, and promoting collaboration and innovation within your team.

Section 3: Building High-Performing Teams

Building high-performing teams is crucial for driving business growth and achieving success. In this section, we will explore strategies for recruiting top talent, nurturing employee growth, and promoting collaboration and innovation within your team. These practices will help you create a cohesive and dynamic team that is motivated, engaged, and capable of delivering exceptional results.

1. **Recruiting Top Talent**

Attracting and hiring the right talent is a fundamental step in building a high-performing team. Consider the following guidance when recruiting top talent:

a. **Clearly Define Job Requirements:** Start by clearly defining the skills, qualifications, and attributes needed for each role. This will help you identify the most suitable candidates. Conduct a thorough analysis of the position's responsibilities and the skills required to excel in that role.

b. **Use Multiple Sourcing Channels:** Utilize a mix of sourcing channels such as job boards, social media platforms, professional networks, and employee referrals to widen your talent pool. Explore niche platforms or industry-specific communities to target candidates with specialized skills or experience.

c. **Craft Compelling Job Descriptions:** Develop engaging and comprehensive job descriptions that accurately depict the role and highlight the unique opportunities and benefits your organization offers. Clearly communicate the organization's values, culture, and growth prospects to attract candidates who align with your vision.

d. **Conduct Structured Interviews:** Develop a structured interview process that includes behavioral-based questions to assess candidates' skills, experiences, and cultural fit. Use a combination of panel interviews, skills assessments, and scenario-based questions to evaluate candidates' abilities to handle real-life situations.

e. **Assess Cultural Fit:** Evaluate candidates' alignment with your organizational values, work culture, and team dynamics. Look for individuals who demonstrate a willingness to collaborate and contribute positively to the team. Consider conducting team interviews or inviting potential candidates for informal meetups with the team to assess compatibility.

2. **Nurturing Employee Growth**

Creating an environment that supports the growth and development of your team members is essential for building a high-performing team. Consider the following guidance:

a. **Provide Opportunities for Learning and Development:** Offer training programs, workshops, and mentorship opportunities to help employees enhance their skills and expand their knowledge. Encourage continuous learning and provide access to resources such as online courses, conferences, and industry events.

b. **Encourage Goal Setting and Personal Development Plans:** Empower employees to set meaningful goals aligned with their aspirations and the organization's objectives. Encourage them to create personal development plans that outline the steps needed to achieve those goals. Regularly review progress and provide support and resources to help them succeed.

c. **Offer Regular Feedback and Performance Reviews:** Provide constructive feedback and conduct regular performance reviews to recognize achievements, address areas for improvement, and provide growth-oriented guidance. Establish a feedback culture that encourages open communication and supports professional development.

d. **Support Career Progression:** Create pathways for career progression within the organization. Offer promotions, new challenges, and opportunities for advancement to motivate and retain talented individuals. Provide mentorship and coaching to help employees develop the skills and competencies needed for future roles.

3. **Promoting Collaboration and Innovation**

Fostering a collaborative and innovative culture is vital for team success. Consider the following guidance:

a. **Establish Open Communication Channels:** Encourage open and transparent communication within the team. Foster an environment where team members feel comfortable sharing ideas, concerns, and feedback. Use collaborative tools and platforms to facilitate communication and information sharing.

b. **Foster a Culture of Trust and Psychological Safety:** Create a safe space where team members feel empowered to take risks, make suggestions, and challenge the status quo without fear of judgment or negative consequences. Encourage constructive dissent and diverse perspectives, recognizing that innovation thrives in an environment where everyone feels heard and valued.

c. **Encourage Cross-Functional Collaboration:** Facilitate collaboration between different departments or teams to foster diverse perspectives, stimulate creativity, and drive innovation. Encourage knowledge sharing and cross-pollination of ideas through cross-functional projects, team-building activities, or regular knowledge-sharing sessions.

d. **Recognize and Reward Innovation:** Acknowledge and reward innovative ideas and initiatives to encourage a culture of innovation and continuous improvement. Celebrate successes and publicly recognize individuals or teams that contribute to the organization's growth through innovative solutions. Implement mechanisms for idea generation, such as suggestion boxes or innovation challenges.

Guidance:

To build high-performing teams, consider the following guidance:

1. **Define Clear Job Requirements:** Clearly articulate the skills, qualifications, and attributes needed for each role to attract the right candidates. Use this information to create job descriptions that accurately reflect the expectations and opportunities within your organization.

2. **Foster a Growth Mindset:** Encourage a growth mindset within your team, emphasizing the importance of continuous learning, improvement, and adaptability. Create a learning culture that encourages curiosity, experimentation, and the pursuit of excellence.

3. **Cultivate a Supportive Work Environment:** Create a supportive and inclusive work environment where employees feel valued, respected, and empowered to contribute their best. Foster a sense of belonging and create opportunities for meaningful connections and collaboration.

4. **Invest In Training and Development:** Provide opportunities for ongoing training and development to enhance employees' skills and capabilities. Offer both technical and soft skills training to ensure a well-rounded team equipped to tackle challenges and seize opportunities.

5. **Embrace Collaboration and Innovation:** Encourage collaboration, idea-sharing, and experimentation to foster a culture of innovation within your team. Provide platforms and resources that facilitate

collaboration and ensure that innovative ideas are recognized and rewarded.

In the next section, we will discuss strategies for nurturing employee growth and development, which includes delegating responsibilities, empowering employees, and creating a culture of accountability. Keep reading!

Section 4: Nurturing Employee Growth and Development

Nurturing employee growth and development is essential for building a high-performing team and driving business growth. In this section, we will explore strategies for delegating responsibilities, empowering employees, and creating a culture of accountability. These practices will help you foster a motivated and engaged workforce that can take on challenges, drive innovation, and achieve collective success.

1. **Delegating Responsibilities**

   Delegating responsibilities is a crucial aspect of effective leadership. It involves assigning tasks and decision-making authority to team members based on their skills, expertise, and development goals. Delegating not only helps distribute workload but also provides individuals with opportunities to learn, take ownership, and showcase their abilities. When delegating, consider the following guidance:

   a. **Assess Employee Skills and Strengths:** Take the time to understand the skills, strengths, and areas of interest of each team member. This will help you identify the right tasks to delegate to individuals who can excel in those areas.

b. **Clearly Communicate Expectations:** Clearly communicate the objectives, desired outcomes, and expectations for delegated tasks. Ensure that employees understand the purpose of the assignment, the level of authority they have, and any relevant deadlines.

c. **Provide Adequate Support and Resources:** Empower employees by providing the necessary support, resources, and training to successfully complete delegated tasks. Ensure they have access to the information, tools, and guidance needed to excel in their responsibilities.

d. **Encourage Autonomy and Decision-Making:** Grant employees the autonomy to make decisions within their delegated responsibilities. Encourage them to think critically, problem-solve, and exercise their judgment. Offer guidance and feedback as needed, while allowing space for them to learn from their experiences.

e. **Recognize and Appreciate Contributions:** Acknowledge and appreciate the efforts and achievements of employees who take on delegated responsibilities. Recognize their contributions publicly, and provide constructive feedback to help them continue to grow and improve.

2. **Empowering Employees**

Empowering employees means giving them the autonomy and authority to make decisions, take initiative, and contribute to the success of the organization. When employees feel empowered, they become more engaged, innovative, and motivated to excel. Here are some strategies for empowering your team:

a. **Provide Opportunities for Skill Development:** Offer training, workshops, seminars, and conferences that align with employees' interests and professional development goals. Encourage them to take advantage of these opportunities to enhance their skills and expand their knowledge.

b. **Delegate Authority and Decision-Making:** Empower employees by granting them the authority and responsibility to make decisions within their roles. Trust their judgment and encourage them to take ownership of their work.

c. **Encourage Innovation and Creativity:** Create an environment that encourages employees to think creatively, share their ideas, and contribute to innovative solutions. Foster an open culture where brainstorming, experimentation, and calculated risk-taking are embraced.

d. **Foster Collaboration and Teamwork:** Encourage collaboration and teamwork among employees by providing opportunities for cross-functional projects, team-building activities, and collaborative problem-solving. Foster a supportive environment where diverse perspectives are valued and teamwork is celebrated.

e. **Offer Mentoring and Coaching:** Assign mentors or coaches to support employees in their professional growth. Encourage regular feedback, coaching sessions, and goal-setting discussions to help employees develop their skills and achieve their career aspirations.

3. Creating a Culture of Accountability

Accountability is vital for driving individual and team performance. When employees feel accountable for their work, they take ownership of their responsibilities, strive for excellence, and demonstrate a strong commitment to achieving results. To foster accountability within your team:

a. **Set Clear Expectations:** Clearly communicate performance expectations, goals, and objectives to employees. Ensure they understand what is expected of them and how their work contributes to the overall success of the team and organization.

b. **Establish Metrics and Key Performance Indicators (KPIs):** Define measurable metrics and KPIs to track individual and team performance. Regularly review progress and provide feedback to help employees stay focused and accountable.

c. **Encourage Self-Reflection and Learning:** Foster a culture of continuous learning and improvement by encouraging employees to reflect on their performance, identify areas for growth, and take proactive steps to enhance their skills and capabilities.

d. **Regularly Provide Feedback:** Offer timely and constructive feedback to employees on their performance, highlighting areas of strength and areas for improvement. Provide guidance and support to help them address challenges and reach their full potential.

e. **Celebrate Achievements and Recognize Effort:** Recognize and celebrate individual and team achievements to reinforce a culture of accountability and motivate employees to excel. Express appreciation for their efforts and acknowledge the value they bring to the organization.

Guidance:

To nurture employee growth and development, consider the following guidance:

1. **Understand Individual Strengths:** Take the time to understand the strengths, skills, and interests of each team member. Delegate responsibilities that align with their abilities to provide opportunities for growth and success.

2. **Provide Support and Resources:** Empower employees by offering the support, resources, and training they need to excel in their roles. Create an environment where they feel supported and have access to the tools and knowledge necessary to perform at their best.

3. **Foster a Learning Culture: Encourage** continuous learning and skill development by providing opportunities for training, mentoring, and coaching. Create a culture where employees are encouraged to seek new knowledge and share their expertise with others.

4. **Encourage Autonomy and Decision-Making:** Grant employees the autonomy to make decisions and take ownership of their work. Trust their judgment and provide guidance and feedback when necessary.

5. **Promote Accountability and Recognition:** Set clear expectations, establish performance metrics, and provide regular feedback to hold employees accountable. Recognize and appreciate their efforts and achievements, fostering a sense of pride and motivation.

By focusing on delegating responsibilities, empowering employees, and creating a culture of accountability, you can nurture the growth and development of your team, leading to enhanced performance, collaboration, and innovation within your organization.

Section 6: Promoting Collaboration and Innovation

Promoting collaboration and innovation is essential for organizations looking to stay competitive and drive business growth. In this section, we will delve deeper into techniques for creating a culture that encourages idea-sharing, cross-functional collaboration, and experimentation. We will also explore the role of effective communication, creating platforms for knowledge exchange, and leveraging technology to facilitate collaboration and drive innovation within your organization.

1. **Creating a Culture of Idea-Sharing**

   In a culture of idea-sharing, employees feel empowered to contribute their unique perspectives and insights. This fosters creativity, sparks innovation, and drives business growth. Consider the following strategies:

   a. **Encouraging Open Dialogue:** Create an environment where open and honest communication is valued. Encourage employees to share their ideas, opinions, and suggestions without fear of judgment or retribution. Regularly schedule team meetings, brainstorming sessions, or idea-sharing forums to provide opportunities for employees to express their thoughts and contribute to discussions.

b. **Establishing Psychological Safety:** Foster a safe and inclusive space where employees feel comfortable expressing unconventional or daring ideas. Emphasize that all contributions are valuable and will be respected and considered. Encourage active listening, empathy, and constructive feedback among team members to create an environment where everyone feels heard and supported.

c. **Rewarding and Recognizing Ideas:** Celebrate and acknowledge individuals or teams who generate innovative ideas. Recognize their contributions publicly, whether through formal rewards or informal recognition, to encourage a culture of idea-sharing. This can include monetary rewards, certificates, or special recognition events to showcase and appreciate the innovative efforts of employees.

2. **Facilitating Cross-Functional Collaboration**

Cross-functional collaboration brings together individuals from different areas of expertise to tackle complex challenges and drive innovation. Consider the following strategies:

a. **Building Collaborative Structures:** Create cross-functional teams or task forces to address specific projects or initiatives. These teams should comprise individuals with diverse skills and knowledge, encouraging collaboration and idea exchange. Assign clear roles and responsibilities to team members and establish effective channels for communication and decision-making.

b. **Encouraging Interdepartmental Communication:** Establish regular communication channels that facilitate knowledge exchange between departments. Encourage employees to seek input and perspectives from colleagues outside their immediate teams. This can be achieved through regular cross-departmental meetings, project updates, or even informal networking events to foster relationships and facilitate collaboration across the organization.

c. **Promoting Shared Goals:** Align departmental objectives with overarching organizational goals to foster collaboration. Emphasize how each team's contribution contributes to the overall success of the business, creating a sense of shared purpose. Establish a clear vision and communicate it consistently to ensure that all employees understand the strategic direction and work towards common objectives.

3. **Leveraging Technology for Collaboration and Innovation**

Technology plays a vital role in enabling effective collaboration and driving innovation. Consider the following strategies:

a. **Utilizing Collaboration Tools:** Implement digital collaboration tools that facilitate communication, document sharing, and project management. These tools enable real-time collaboration, even for remote or geographically dispersed teams. Examples include project management platforms, shared document repositories, and instant messaging applications.

b. **Encouraging Virtual Collaboration:** Embrace virtual meeting platforms, instant messaging applications, and project management software to facilitate collaboration among employees working in different locations or time zones. Ensure that employees have access to reliable technology and resources to effectively collaborate virtually.

c. **Creating Knowledge-Sharing Platforms:** Establish centralized platforms for knowledge sharing, such as intranets, wikis, or digital libraries. Encourage employees to share their expertise, best practices, and lessons learned to foster a culture of continuous learning and innovation. Consider implementing gamification elements, such as badges or leaderboards, to incentivize knowledge sharing and engagement.

d. **Leveraging Social Media and Enterprise Social Networks:** Utilize social media platforms or internal enterprise social networks to encourage idea-sharing, collaboration, and knowledge exchange. These platforms can facilitate networking, brainstorming, and the discovery of new insights and perspectives. Encourage employees to actively participate in relevant industry forums or online communities to stay updated on the latest trends and developments.

Guidance:

To promote collaboration and innovation within your organization, consider the following guidance:

1. **Leadership Support:** Leadership plays a crucial role in creating a culture of collaboration and innovation. Encourage leaders to actively participate in cross-functional projects, lead by example, and provide resources and support for collaborative initiatives. Foster an environment where leaders value and solicit input from team members at all levels.

2. **Training and Development:** Offer training programs and workshops that focus on building collaborative skills, effective communication, and creative problem-solving. Provide employees with the tools and knowledge they need to collaborate effectively,

such as conflict resolution training, negotiation skills development, or creativity and innovation workshops.

3. **Break Down Silos:** Actively work to break down departmental or hierarchical barriers that hinder collaboration. Encourage collaboration between different teams, departments, and levels of the organization. Foster a culture of sharing and openness where individuals from diverse backgrounds can come together to solve complex challenges.

4. **Encourage Experimentation:** Foster a culture that embraces experimentation and tolerates reasonable risk-taking. Encourage employees to test new ideas, learn from failures, and iterate on their approaches. Provide a supportive environment where mistakes are viewed as learning opportunities rather than failures.

5. **Emphasize Continuous Improvement:** Promote a mindset of continuous improvement and learning. Encourage employees to reflect on past projects, share learnings, and apply insights to future initiatives. Implement mechanisms for gathering feedback, conducting post-project reviews, and implementing lessons learned to drive ongoing improvement and innovation.

Here are two real-world examples of businesses that achieved growth through effective leadership and team development:

Google:

Google is widely recognized as a company that prioritizes effective leadership and team development. The company's success can be attributed to its focus on cultivating a culture of innovation and collaboration. Google encourages its employees to take risks, explore new ideas, and contribute to projects outside their immediate roles. The company's "20% time" policy allows employees to dedicate a portion of their workweek to personal projects, fostering creativity and promoting cross-functional collaboration. By investing in leadership development programs, Google ensures that its managers are equipped with the necessary skills to support their teams and drive performance. This emphasis on leadership and team development has played a significant role in Google's growth and its reputation as an industry leader.

Zappos:

Zappos, an online shoe and clothing retailer, is known for its strong emphasis on employee growth and development. The company places a high value on its core values, including "Deliver WOW through service" and "Create fun and a little weirdness." Zappos recognizes that engaged and empowered employees are essential for delivering exceptional customer service and driving business growth. The company invests in training and development programs to help employees enhance their skills, develop their careers, and align with the company's culture. Zappos also fosters a supportive and inclusive work environment, encouraging employees to express their ideas, collaborate, and embrace innovation. By nurturing a strong sense of team spirit and providing opportunities for growth, Zappos has been able to create a loyal and motivated workforce, leading to business growth and success.

These examples highlight how effective leadership and team development can contribute to the growth and success of organizations. By investing in their employees, fostering a positive work culture, and promoting collaboration and innovation, businesses can achieve remarkable outcomes and maintain a competitive edge in their respective industries.

Conclusion

In conclusion, strong leadership and effective team development are crucial elements in driving business growth. By developing leadership skills, fostering a positive work culture, building high-performing teams, nurturing employee growth, promoting collaboration and innovation, and creating a culture of accountability, organizations can unlock their full potential and achieve sustainable growth. In the next chapter, we will explore the importance of strategic planning and execution in realizing business goals and driving success.

Part 6: Overcoming Growth Obstacles

Chapter 9: Overcoming Growth Challenges

---◦◊◦---

Introduction

As businesses strive for growth and expansion, they often encounter a myriad of challenges and obstacles along their journey. In Chapter 9, we will delve into the complex landscape of overcoming growth challenges and provide valuable insights and strategies to navigate them successfully. This chapter aims to equip business leaders and entrepreneurs with the knowledge and tools to address scalability issues, manage increased complexity, adapt to changing market dynamics, mitigate risks, and maintain business continuity.

Growth brings exciting opportunities, but it also presents unique challenges that can impede progress if not effectively managed. By understanding and anticipating these challenges, businesses can proactively develop strategies to overcome them and continue their growth trajectory. This chapter will serve as a practical guide, offering actionable advice and real-world examples to empower readers in their quest for sustained growth and success.

Section 1: Addressing Scalability Issues

During periods of growth, businesses often encounter scalability issues that can hinder their progress and expansion. Scalability refers to the ability of a business to handle increasing demands and expand its operations without compromising efficiency or quality. In this section, we will explore common challenges and obstacles associated with scalability and provide guidance on how to address them effectively.

1. Managing Increasing Workload

    As a business grows, the workload tends to increase significantly. This can strain existing resources and processes, leading to inefficiencies and potential bottlenecks.

    To address this challenge, consider the following strategies:

    a. **Streamline Processes:** Conduct a thorough analysis of your business processes to identify areas where efficiency can be improved. Look for opportunities to eliminate redundant tasks, automate repetitive processes, and optimize resource allocation. Implementing lean principles and continuous improvement practices can help streamline workflows and increase productivity.

    b. **Delegate and Empower:** As the workloads increase, it's crucial to delegate responsibilities to capable team members. Empower your employees to make decisions and take ownership of their tasks. Establish clear lines of authority and accountability to ensure efficient task allocation and decision-making. This not only lightens the load on leaders but also fosters a sense of ownership and empowerment within the team.

    c. **Invest in Technology:** Scaling your business often requires investing in scalable technologies and systems that can handle increasing workloads.

Evaluate your existing technology infrastructure and identify areas where upgrades or new solutions can improve efficiency and productivity. This may include adopting cloud-based solutions for storage and collaboration, implementing project management tools, or leveraging automation software to streamline repetitive tasks.

2. **Expanding Infrastructure and Resources**

Business growth often requires expanding physical infrastructure, such as production facilities, warehouses, or office spaces. It also necessitates acquiring additional resources, including human capital and equipment.

Here are some considerations to effectively address these challenges:

a. **Plan Ahead:** Anticipate future growth and plan infrastructure expansion accordingly. Conduct feasibility studies to assess capacity requirements and identify potential bottlenecks. Develop a comprehensive growth plan that outlines the necessary steps, timelines, and resource requirements to avoid delays and disruptions.

b. **Strategic Partnerships:** Consider forming strategic partnerships with other businesses or suppliers to leverage their existing infrastructure and resources. Joint ventures or outsourcing arrangements can provide cost-effective and scalable solutions. Collaborating with partners who specialize in areas where your business lacks expertise or capacity can help expedite growth and mitigate resource constraints.

c. **Financing Options**: Expanding infrastructure and acquiring resources often require significant financial investment. Explore financing options to fund these growth initiatives. This may involve traditional methods such as loans or seeking investment from venture capitalists. Additionally, alternative financing options like crowdfunding or grants may be available depending on your industry and growth objectives.

3. **Scaling Product and Service Offerings**

As demand increases, businesses may face challenges in scaling their product or service offerings to meet customer needs effectively.

Consider the following strategies to address these challenges:

a. **Standardize Processes:** Implement standardized procedures and best practices to ensure consistency and quality across products or services. This allows for easier replication and scalability as your business expands. Documenting and optimizing key processes can help streamline operations and maintain quality standards.

b. **Prioritize Customer Feedback:** Actively listen to customer feedback and use it to refine and enhance your offerings. Regularly collect and analyze customer insights to understand their evolving needs and preferences. Incorporate this feedback into your product development roadmap to ensure your offerings remain relevant and aligned with customer expectations.

c. **Agile Product Development:** Adopt an agile approach to product development, allowing for iterative improvements and faster time-to-market. Breaking down development into smaller, manageable cycles enables you to respond swiftly to market demands and scale your offerings accordingly. Embrace feedback loops and involve customers in the development process through beta testing or early access programs.

By addressing scalability issues proactively, businesses can overcome growth challenges and position themselves for sustainable expansion. It is essential to continually reassess and optimize processes, invest in infrastructure and resources, and adapt offerings to meet the evolving demands of the market. Embracing scalability as a core focus will enable businesses to navigate growth periods successfully and seize new opportunities for long-term success.

Section 3: Mitigating Risks and Addressing Resource Constraints

During periods of growth, businesses often encounter various risks and resource constraints that can hinder their progress. It is crucial to proactively identify and address these challenges to ensure the continued success and sustainability of your business. In this section, we will delve deeper into effective strategies for mitigating risks and effectively managing resource limitations.

1. **Identifying and Assessing Risks**

a. **Conduct a comprehensive risk assessment:** Begin by conducting a thorough analysis of your business processes, market conditions, competitive landscape, and external factors that may influence your operations. This assessment will help you identify potential risks and their potential impact on your business. By gaining a clear understanding of the risks, you can prioritize and allocate resources effectively to manage and mitigate them.

b. **Prioritize risks:** Once you have identified the potential risks, prioritize them based on their likelihood and potential impact on your business. This prioritization will enable you to focus your efforts and resources on the risks that pose the greatest threat. Develop a risk mitigation plan that outlines specific actions and strategies for addressing each identified risk. Regularly review and update this plan as new risks emerge or existing ones evolve.

2. **Developing a Resource Optimization Plan**

a. **Evaluate your existing resources:** Conduct a comprehensive evaluation of your financial, human, and physical resources. Identify areas where resources may be limited or underutilized. This analysis will help you identify opportunities for optimization and reallocation of resources to areas where they can have the most significant impact.

b. **Implement cost-cutting measures:** Identify areas where you can reduce costs without compromising the quality of your products or services. This may involve renegotiating contracts with suppliers, streamlining operational processes, or eliminating unnecessary expenses. Look for ways to improve efficiency and eliminate waste throughout your organization.

c. **Explore alternative funding sources**: If you are facing financial constraints, consider exploring alternative funding sources such as loans, grants, or partnerships. Research government programs, venture capital firms, and other potential sources of funding that align with your business goals. This can provide you with the necessary resources to support your growth initiatives and overcome resource limitations.

3. **Prioritizing and Streamlining Operations**

   a. **Evaluate and optimize business processes:** Review your business processes and identify areas where improvements can be made. Look for opportunities to eliminate redundancies, automate repetitive tasks, or outsource non-core activities. Streamlining operations will improve efficiency, reduce costs, and allow you to allocate resources more effectively to drive growth.

   b. **Focus on core competencies:** Identify your core competencies and focus on developing and leveraging them. By concentrating on what you do best, you can optimize your resources and deliver exceptional value to your customers. Outsourcing non-core functions to external experts or strategic partners can help you allocate resources more efficiently and free up internal resources for core activities.

4. **Building Strategic Alliances**

   a. **Identify potential partners:** Look for businesses or organizations that complement your products, services, or target market. Identify potential partners with whom you can collaborate to share resources, expertise, and market access. Consider forming strategic alliances, joint ventures, or partnerships that can provide mutual benefits and help overcome resource limitations.

b. **Establish clear agreements:** When entering strategic alliances, ensure that the roles, responsibilities, and expectations of each partner are clearly defined. Establish clear agreements and contracts that outline the terms of collaboration, resource sharing, and mutual benefits. Regularly communicate and collaborate with your partners to ensure alignment and maximize the value of the partnership.

5. **Implementing Effective Risk Management Practices**

    a. **Establish a risk management framework:** Develop a comprehensive risk management framework and processes within your organization. This includes identifying risks, assessing their potential impact, and developing mitigation strategies. Assign responsibility for risk management to qualified individuals within your team and establish clear protocols for risk monitoring and reporting.

    b. **Continuously monitor and assess risks:** Regularly monitor and assess both internal and external factors that may impact your business. Stay updated on market trends, regulatory changes, and other developments that could affect your operations. Adjust your risk management strategies as needed to adapt to changing circumstances. Foster a culture of continuous improvement and learning, where risk awareness and mitigation are embedded in the decision-making process.

    c. **Foster a risk-aware culture:** Encourage a culture of risk awareness and accountability within your organization. Educate employees about potential risks and provide training on risk management practices. Empower employees to proactively identify and report potential risks, fostering a proactive and vigilant approach to risk management. Encourage open communication and collaboration across teams to foster a shared understanding of risks and their potential impact on the business.

By implementing these strategies, you can effectively mitigate risks and address resource constraints to navigate growth challenges successfully. However, it is important to note that every business is unique, and the specific strategies you employ should be tailored to your organization's needs and circumstances. Seeking professional advice and engaging with industry experts can provide valuable insights and guidance for managing risks and optimizing resources during periods of growth.

Section 4: Implementing Effective Risk Management Practices

Implementing effective risk management practices is crucial for businesses to proactively identify, assess, and mitigate potential risks that may arise during periods of growth. Risk management involves identifying uncertainties that could impact the achievement of business objectives and taking appropriate actions to minimize their potential negative impact. In this section, we will explore the importance of risk management and provide detailed guidance on implementing effective risk management practices.

1. **Understanding the Importance of Risk Management:**

   Risk management is a fundamental aspect of business growth and sustainability. It helps businesses navigate the uncertainties and challenges that come with expansion and ensures that potential risks are identified and addressed in a proactive manner.

Effective risk management allows businesses to:

a. **Minimize financial losses:** By identifying and mitigating risks, businesses can avoid or minimize the financial losses that could result from unforeseen events or circumstances. This includes risks related to market fluctuations, regulatory changes, operational disruptions, and more.

b. **Protect reputation and brand value:** A strong reputation is crucial for business success. Effective risk management helps businesses safeguard their reputation by addressing potential risks that could harm their brand image, customer trust, or stakeholder relationships. It allows businesses to respond quickly and effectively to any negative events or crises.

c. **Enhance decision-making:** Risk management provides valuable insights into potential risks and their potential impact on business objectives. It enables informed decision-making by considering risk factors, weighing potential outcomes, and selecting the most appropriate strategies for growth and expansion.

d. **Ensure business continuity:** By identifying and planning for potential risks, businesses can develop strategies to ensure continuity even in the face of unexpected events. This includes having contingency plans, business continuity plans, and disaster recovery plans in place to minimize disruptions and maintain operations during challenging times.

2. **Identify and Assess Risks:**

The first step in effective risk management is to identify and assess the various risks that may impact your business. This involves a systematic process of identifying potential risks, evaluating their likelihood and potential impact, and prioritizing them based on their significance.

Key considerations in this step include:

a. **Conducting a comprehensive risk assessment:** Engage with stakeholders, including employees, customers, suppliers, and industry experts, to identify potential risks across different areas of your business, such as operational, financial, legal, regulatory, and reputational risks. Consider both internal and external factors that could affect your business.

b. **Assessing risk likelihood and impact:** Once risks are identified, evaluate their likelihood of occurrence and the potential impact they could have on your business. This assessment can be qualitative or quantitative, depending on the nature of the risks. Assign risk ratings based on the probability and severity of each risk to prioritize your focus and allocate resources accordingly.

c. **Considering emerging risks:** In addition to known risks, it is important to consider emerging risks that may arise due to changing market dynamics, technological advancements, or other external factors. Stay informed about industry trends, regulatory changes, and emerging threats to ensure your risk management strategies are up-to-date and relevant.

3. Develop Risk Mitigation Strategies

Once risks are identified and assessed, the next step is to develop risk mitigation strategies that minimize the potential negative impact on your business. This involves implementing measures to prevent risks from occurring, reducing their likelihood and impact, or effectively managing them if they materialize.

Key considerations in this step include:

a. **Risk prevention and reduction:** Implement measures to prevent risks from occurring or reduce their likelihood and impact. This may involve improving operational processes, implementing robust security measures, diversifying suppliers or markets, or enhancing quality control systems. Address the root causes of risks to minimize their occurrence.

b. **Risk transfer and sharing:** Explore options for transferring or sharing risks with external parties. This can be done through insurance coverage, contractual agreements, or partnerships. Transferring certain risks to specialized service providers or sharing responsibilities with strategic partners can help mitigate the financial impact and provide additional expertise and support.

c. **Risk acceptance and contingency planning:** Some risks may be unavoidable or have a low likelihood of occurrence but high potential impact. In such cases, develop contingency plans to effectively manage the risks if they materialize. Identify alternative courses of action, establish backup plans, and allocate resources to mitigate the impact of these risks on your business.

4. **Implement Risk Management Processes**

   To ensure effective risk management, it is essential to establish clear processes and protocols within your organization. This includes:

   a. **Assigning responsibility:** Designate individuals or teams responsible for risk management within your organization. Clearly define their roles and responsibilities, ensuring they have the necessary expertise and authority to carry out risk management activities effectively. Foster a culture of ownership and accountability for risk management throughout the organization.

   b. **Establishing risk monitoring mechanisms:** Implement processes for ongoing risk monitoring and reporting. Regularly review and update risk assessments, track key risk indicators, and establish early warning systems to identify emerging risks. Continuously monitor changes in the business environment and update risk management strategies and plans accordingly.

   c. **Communicating and documenting risks:** Establish effective communication channels to ensure that relevant stakeholders are aware of identified risks and the corresponding mitigation strategies. Document risks, mitigation plans, and any actions taken to manage risks. This documentation serves as a valuable resource for future reference and provides insights for future risk assessments and decision-making.

5. **Embedding a Risk-Aware Culture**

Building a risk-aware culture is critical for successful risk management. This involves fostering an organizational environment where risk awareness and mitigation are embedded in daily operations.

Key considerations in promoting a risk-aware culture include:

a. **Employee engagement and training:** Involve employees at all levels in the risk management process. Provide training and awareness programs to educate employees about risks, their potential impact, and the actions they can take to mitigate them. Encourage open communication and create a supportive environment where employees feel comfortable reporting potential risks and suggesting improvements.

b. **Regular risk reviews and updates:** Conduct regular reviews of risk management processes, strategies, and their effectiveness. Foster a culture of continuous improvement by encouraging feedback and incorporating lessons learned from previous risk events. Regularly update risk assessments, risk registers, and mitigation plans based on new information and changing business dynamics.

c. **Leadership commitment:** Leadership plays a crucial role in driving a risk-aware culture. Demonstrate your commitment to risk management by leading by example, making risk-informed decisions, and allocating resources to support risk management initiatives. Communicate the importance of risk management and its alignment with the overall business strategy to instill a sense of urgency and ownership among employees.

By implementing these effective risk management practices, businesses can proactively identify and address potential risks, ensuring the resilience and success of their growth journey. Remember that risk management is an ongoing process that requires continuous evaluation, adaptation, and vigilance as your business evolves and the external environment changes.

Real-life examples and case studies of businesses that successfully navigated growth challenges can provide valuable insights and inspiration for others. Let's explore a few notable examples:

1. **Amazon**

   Amazon, originally an online bookstore, faced significant growth challenges as it expanded its product offerings and became a global e-commerce giant. One of the key challenges it encountered was managing its logistics and supply chain operations to meet the increasing customer demands. To address this challenge, Amazon invested heavily in building sophisticated fulfillment centers and implementing advanced inventory management systems. Through continuous innovation and technology-driven solutions, Amazon transformed its logistics operations and created a seamless customer experience, enabling its growth into various product categories and international markets.

2. **Netflix**

   Netflix, a leading streaming service provider, experienced rapid growth as it transitioned from a DVD-by-mail service to an online streaming platform. During this transformation, the company faced challenges related to content licensing, competition, and shifting consumer preferences. To overcome these challenges,

Netflix invested in original content production, securing exclusive distribution rights, and leveraging data analytics to personalize user recommendations. By adapting its business model and focusing on customer-centric strategies, Netflix not only navigated the growth challenges but also revolutionized the entertainment industry.

3. **Airbnb**

As a peer-to-peer online marketplace for accommodation, Airbnb disrupted the traditional hospitality industry. However, its growth was accompanied by challenges related to regulatory compliance, safety concerns, and maintaining quality standards. To address these challenges, Airbnb worked closely with governments and implemented robust safety protocols, including enhanced identity verification and customer reviews. By proactively engaging with stakeholders and demonstrating a commitment to addressing concerns, Airbnb not only overcame regulatory hurdles but also built trust among users and hosts, leading to sustained growth and global expansion.

4. **Tesla**

Tesla, an electric vehicle manufacturer, faced numerous challenges as it aimed to disrupt the automotive industry. From establishing a reliable supply chain for batteries to building a network of charging stations and educating consumers about electric vehicles, Tesla encountered obstacles at every stage of its growth journey. However, through innovative product design, superior performance, and a relentless focus on sustainability, Tesla successfully positioned itself as a leader in the electric vehicle market. The company's commitment to continuous innovation, coupled with strong leadership, has enabled it to navigate challenges and achieve remarkable growth.

These real-life examples highlight the importance of agility, innovation, and strategic decision-making in overcoming growth challenges. By learning from their experiences, businesses can gain valuable insights and apply relevant strategies to their own growth journeys. It is crucial to adapt and evolve in response to changing market dynamics, anticipate and address potential obstacles, and maintain a customer-centric approach to drive sustainable growth.

Conclusion

In conclusion, navigating growth challenges is an integral part of building a successful and sustainable business. Throughout this chapter, we have explored the common obstacles and complexities that businesses encounter during periods of growth, and we have provided strategies and guidance to overcome them.

We emphasized the importance of addressing scalability issues to ensure that a business can expand efficiently without compromising quality or customer experience. Managing increased complexity requires effective leadership, streamlined processes, and the ability to adapt to changing market dynamics.

Mitigating risks and implementing sound risk management practices is crucial for maintaining business continuity and protecting against potential setbacks. By identifying and managing risks proactively, businesses can confidently pursue growth opportunities while safeguarding their operations.

Additionally, we discussed the significance of strategic resource allocation and optimizing financial resources to support growth initiatives. Managing finances effectively, securing funding, and implementing financial planning and budgeting practices are essential for sustainable growth.

Lastly, we explored real-life examples and case studies of businesses that successfully navigated growth challenges. These examples demonstrate the importance of agility, innovation, and strong leadership in overcoming obstacles and emerging stronger.

As you continue your growth journey, it is vital to embrace challenges as opportunities for learning and improvement. By adopting the strategies and insights shared in this chapter, you can position your business for success and effectively overcome the hurdles that come with growth.

Now, let's turn our attention to Chapter 10: Growing Your Business: A Blueprint for Success. In this final chapter, we will summarize the key lessons and strategies discussed throughout the book and provide you with a comprehensive blueprint for growing your business. We will highlight the essential steps and considerations that will empower you to develop your own growth plans and strategies.

As you embark on this final chapter, remember the importance of perseverance, agility, and a customer-centric approach in achieving sustainable business expansion. Use the knowledge you have gained from this book to fuel your growth journey and make informed decisions that will propel your business to new heights.

Get ready to transform your business and unlock its full potential as we dive into Chapter 10: Growing Your Business: A Blueprint for Success.

Part 7: Blueprint for Success

Chapter 10: Growing Your Business: A Blueprint for Success

---◦◇◦---

Introduction

As we reach the final chapter of this book, it is time to bring together all the valuable insights and strategies we have explored thus far. Throughout the preceding chapters, we have delved into various aspects of business growth and expansion, learning essential lessons and uncovering effective strategies. Now, let's synthesize this knowledge into a comprehensive blueprint for growing your business.

Section 1: Summarizing Key Lessons and Strategies

Throughout this book, we have explored a wealth of valuable insights and strategies for driving business growth and achieving sustainable success.

Let's take a moment to summarize the key lessons and strategies we have discussed:

1. **Vision and Strategic Goals:** We have learned that a clear vision and strategic goals are fundamental to business growth. By defining your long-term vision and setting specific, measurable, achievable, relevant, and time-bound (SMART) goals, you

provide your business with a clear direction and purpose.

2. **Market Analysis and Customer-Centric Approach:** Understanding your target market and customers is essential for business growth. Conducting thorough market analysis helps you identify market trends, consumer preferences, and unmet needs. By adopting a customer-centric approach, you can tailor your products or services to meet those needs and gain a competitive advantage.

3. **Effective Marketing and Customer Acquisition:** We have explored the importance of effective marketing in driving business growth. From branding and messaging to positioning and targeting, every aspect of your marketing strategy plays a crucial role. Leveraging various marketing channels and tactics, such as digital marketing, social media, content marketing, and partnerships, helps you reach and acquire new customers.

4. **Customer Retention and Loyalty:** Retaining existing customers is equally vital as acquiring new ones. We have discussed customer retention strategies, including loyalty programs, personalized experiences, and exceptional customer service. By nurturing strong relationships with your customers and providing ongoing value, you can foster loyalty and turn them into brand advocates.

5. **Strategic Partnerships:** Strategic partnerships can fuel business growth and expansion. We explored different types of partnerships, such as joint ventures, distribution agreements, and co-marketing initiatives. By identifying and selecting

the right partners, negotiating partnerships, and managing collaborations effectively, you can tap into new markets, access additional resources, and leverage complementary expertise.

6. **Innovation and Adaptation:** Innovation and adaptation are crucial for staying competitive and driving growth. We discussed techniques for fostering a culture of innovation, encouraging creative thinking, and embracing change. By continuously identifying market trends, anticipating customer needs, and developing innovative products or services, you can stay ahead of the curve and meet evolving demands.

7. **Financial Management:** Effective financial management is essential for sustainable growth. We explored strategies for managing cash flow, securing funding, and optimizing financial resources. Financial planning, budgeting, and forecasting help you make informed decisions and allocate resources efficiently.

8. **Leadership and Team Development:** Strong leadership and high-performing teams are the backbone of successful businesses. We delved into techniques for developing leadership skills, fostering a positive work culture, and building teams that thrive. Recruiting top talent, nurturing employee growth, and promoting collaboration and innovation are key strategies for building a cohesive and motivated workforce.

By internalizing these key lessons and strategies, you are equipped with a comprehensive toolkit for driving business growth. These insights serve as a foundation for the comprehensive blueprint we will outline in the subsequent sections of this chapter, guiding you through the essential steps and considerations for growing your business.

Section 2: A Comprehensive Blueprint for Growing Your Business

To achieve sustainable growth and success, it is essential to follow a well-defined blueprint. This blueprint outlines the essential steps and considerations for growing your business effectively.

Let's explore each component in detail:

1. **Refine Your Vision and Goals:** Start by refining your vision and strategic goals. Clarify your long-term vision and define specific, measurable, achievable, relevant, and time-bound (SMART) goals. These goals will serve as guiding principles for your growth journey and provide a clear direction for your business.

2. **Conduct Thorough Market Analysis:** Continuously analyze your target market and stay abreast of market trends, customer preferences, and emerging opportunities. Conduct thorough market research to understand your customers' needs, behaviors, and pain points. This knowledge will help you identify gaps in the market and develop innovative solutions to meet customer demands.

3. **Develop a Customer-Centric Approach:** Place your customers at the heart of your business. Strive to understand their needs, preferences, and aspirations. Tailor your products or services to

provide unique value and exceptional experiences. Implement a customer feedback system to gather insights and continuously improve your offerings.

4. **Build an Effective Marketing Strategy:** Craft an effective marketing strategy that aligns with your target audience and business goals. Develop a strong brand identity, messaging, and positioning that resonates with your customers. Leverage various marketing channels, such as digital marketing, social media, content marketing, and partnerships, to reach and engage your target market effectively.

5. **Foster Innovation and Adaptation:** Cultivate a culture of innovation and adaptability within your organization. Encourage creative thinking, experimentation, and continuous learning. Stay agile and responsive to changing market dynamics. Regularly assess your product or service offerings, and seek opportunities for improvement and differentiation.

6. **Optimize Financial Management:** Implement sound financial management practices to support your growth objectives. Continuously monitor and manage your cash flow, ensuring it aligns with your business operations and growth plans. Seek funding options that align with your business needs, such as loans, investments, or grants. Optimize your financial resources to maximize growth potential.

7. **Develop Strong Leadership and Teamwork:** Invest in developing strong leadership skills and fostering teamwork. Empower your leaders to inspire and motivate their teams. Nurture a positive work

culture that encourages collaboration, open communication, and shared goals. Provide professional development opportunities to enhance the skills and capabilities of your employees.

8. **Implement Performance Monitoring and Optimization:** Establish key performance indicators (KPIs) to measure the success of your growth strategies. Continuously monitor and analyze your business performance, and identify areas for improvement. Regularly review your strategies and adapt them based on data-driven insights.

9. **Cultivate Strategic Partnerships:** Forge strategic partnerships that complement your business objectives and expand your market reach. Collaborate with like-minded organizations, suppliers, distributors, or industry influencers to leverage their expertise, resources, and networks. Establish mutually beneficial relationships that drive mutual growth and create new opportunities.

10. **Embrace Change and Continuous Improvement:** Remain adaptable and embrace change as a fundamental aspect of growth. Encourage a culture of continuous improvement and learning within your organization. Stay informed about industry trends, technological advancements, and evolving customer needs. Adapt your strategies, processes, and products/services accordingly to stay ahead of the competition.

By following this comprehensive blueprint, you can navigate the intricacies of business growth and set a solid foundation for long-term success. Remember, each business is unique, so tailor the blueprint to your specific circumstances and continually iterate based on feedback and market insights.

Section 3: Applying the Knowledge: Developing Your Growth Plans and Strategies

Now that you have gained valuable insights and knowledge from this book, it's time to apply them to develop your own growth plans and strategies.

Follow these steps to create a well-defined roadmap for your business expansion:

1. **Assess Your Current Position:** Begin by assessing your current business position. Evaluate your strengths, weaknesses, opportunities, and threats (SWOT analysis). This analysis will help you identify areas where you can leverage your strengths and address areas that need improvement.

2. **Define Your Growth Objectives:** Clearly define your growth objectives based on your long-term vision and SMART goals. Consider both quantitative and qualitative objectives, such as revenue targets, market share expansion, customer satisfaction improvement, or product/service innovation.

3. **Identify Growth Opportunities:** Based on your market analysis and customer insights, identify growth opportunities that align with your objectives. Look for untapped market segments, emerging trends, or potential partnerships that can propel your business forward. Consider both organic growth (expanding existing offerings) and inorganic

growth (acquiring new businesses or entering new markets).

4. **Develop Actionable Strategies:** Translate your growth objectives and identified opportunities into actionable strategies. Break down your strategies into specific initiatives and projects that will drive growth. Consider different aspects of your business, such as marketing, sales, product development, operations, and customer service, to develop a holistic approach.

5. **Allocate Resources:** Determine the resources required to execute your growth strategies effectively. This includes financial resources, personnel, technology, and infrastructure. Prioritize resource allocation based on the potential impact and feasibility of each strategy.

6. **Create Implementation Timelines:** Establish realistic timelines for implementing each strategy and initiative. Break down your timelines into manageable phases or milestones to track progress effectively. Assign responsibilities and establish accountability for each task or project.

7. **Monitor and Measure Progress:** Put in place systems to monitor and measure the progress of your growth plans. Define key performance indicators (KPIs) that align with your objectives and regularly track them. Use data and analytics to evaluate the effectiveness of your strategies and make data-driven adjustments when necessary.

8. **Foster a Culture of Adaptability and Learning:** Encourage a culture of adaptability and continuous learning within your organization. Embrace

feedback and learn from both successes and failures. Promote collaboration and cross-functional teamwork to foster innovation and creative problem-solving.

9. **Seek Expert Guidance and Mentorship:** Consider seeking expert guidance and mentorship from experienced professionals or business consultants. They can provide valuable insights, guidance, and industry-specific knowledge to help you navigate growth challenges more effectively.

10. **Stay Committed and Persevere:** Growth is a journey that requires dedication, commitment, and perseverance. Be prepared to face obstacles and setbacks along the way. Stay focused on your long-term vision and maintain the agility to adapt and adjust your plans as needed.

By applying the knowledge gained from this book and following these steps, you can develop a comprehensive growth plan and strategies that align with your business objectives. Remember, the journey of growth requires continuous evaluation, learning, and refinement. Stay agile, be open to feedback, and embrace the opportunities that arise as you strive for sustainable business expansion.

Section 4: Perseverance, Agility, and a Customer-Centric Approach

As you embark on your journey of business growth, it's crucial to embrace certain principles that will drive your success.

These principles include perseverance, agility, and a customer-centric approach. Let's explore each of these in more detail:

1. **Perseverance:** Growth is rarely a linear path. It requires resilience, determination, and the ability to overcome challenges. Be prepared to face obstacles, setbacks, and moments of doubt. Perseverance is about staying committed to your vision and goals, even when the road gets tough. It means learning from failures, adapting your strategies, and continuing to move forward despite adversity. Remember that every successful business has encountered obstacles along the way, and it is through perseverance that they have emerged stronger.

2. **Agility:** In today's rapidly changing business landscape, agility is crucial for sustained growth. Agility means being responsive, flexible, and adaptable to market dynamics and emerging trends. It requires a willingness to embrace change, take calculated risks, and quickly adjust your strategies based on new information. By staying agile, you can seize opportunities, mitigate risks, and effectively navigate the evolving business landscape. Embrace a culture that encourages experimentation, innovation, and continuous improvement to foster agility within your organization.

3. **Customer-Centric Approach:** Customers are at the heart of your business, and a customer-centric approach is vital for sustainable growth. Understand your customers' needs, preferences, and pain points. Continuously gather feedback and insights to refine your products, services, and customer

experience. Create personalized and meaningful interactions that build strong relationships and foster loyalty. Invest in customer service and support, going above and beyond to exceed expectations. By putting the customer at the center of your decision-making and operations, you will create a strong foundation for growth.

These principles—perseverance, agility, and a customer-centric approach—should be deeply ingrained in your organization's culture. They should guide your decision-making processes, influence how you respond to challenges, and shape your interactions with customers and employees alike. By embodying these principles, you can navigate the complexities of business growth with confidence and drive sustainable success.

As you embark on your growth journey, remember that the blueprint outlined in this book provides a framework for your success. However, every business is unique, and it's important to tailor these strategies to fit your specific circumstances. Continuously evaluate, learn, and refine your approach as you progress.

Now, armed with the knowledge and guidance from this book, it's time for you to take action. Apply the lessons learned, leverage the strategies discussed, and adapt them to your business's unique needs. Create your own blueprint for success and make it a living document that evolves with your business. Stay committed, embrace change, and keep your customers at the forefront of everything you do.

Congratulations on embarking on this exciting journey of growth. With perseverance, agility, and a customer-centric approach, you have the tools to achieve remarkable success.

Part 8: Resources and Further Exploration

Chapter 11: Resources for Further Exploration

---•◇•°---

Introduction

In the journey of scaling and sustaining business expansion, continuous learning and exploration are essential. This chapter serves as a valuable resource guide, offering a curated list of additional resources to deepen your knowledge and enhance your understanding of growth strategies, entrepreneurship, leadership, and business management. Here, you will find recommended books, articles, websites, online courses, professional organizations, and conferences that can provide valuable insights, industry-specific knowledge, and networking opportunities to fuel your growth ambitions.

Whether you're seeking to refine your leadership skills, explore innovative business models, or gain industry-specific expertise, these resources will serve as valuable companions on your growth journey. Additionally, we will highlight relevant government programs, grants, and funding opportunities that can support your business expansion plans.

Each resource is carefully selected to provide practical guidance, real-world case studies, and actionable insights. We will provide a brief description or review for each resource, highlighting its value and relevance to your scaling efforts. By exploring these resources, you'll have access to a wealth of knowledge and a network of like-minded individuals who can inspire and support you in achieving sustainable business growth.

We encourage you to leverage these resources to further your understanding, connect with industry experts, and develop a robust toolkit for success. The power to drive your business forward lies in continuous learning, exploration, and the application of new insights. Embrace the opportunity to expand your horizons and unlock the full potential of your business.

Now, let's dive into the rich array of resources that await you, empowering you to chart a path of growth and prosperity.

Section 1: Additional Resources for Scaling and Sustaining Business Expansion

As you continue your journey of scaling and sustaining business expansion, it's important to continually expand your knowledge and stay updated with the latest insights and best practices. To support your learning, here is a curated list of additional resources that you can explore:

1. **Books:**

    - *"Scaling Up: How a Few Companies Make It...and Why the Rest Don't"* by Verne Harnish

    - *"The Lean Startup: How Today's Entrepreneurs Use Continuous Innovation to Create Radically Successful Businesses"* by Eric Ries

    - *"The Innovator's Dilemma: When New Technologies Cause Great Firms to Fail"* by Clayton M. Christensen

    - *"Good to Great: Why Some Companies Make the Leap...and Others Don't"* by Jim Collins

- *"The Startup Owner's Manual: The Step-by-Step Guide for Building a Great Company"* by Steve Blank and Bob Dorf

- *"Starting Strong Mastering the Fundamentals of Launching a Successful Venture"* by Reginald Johnson

- *"Funding Your Vision Strategies and Resources for Financing Business Growth"* by Reginald Johnson

2. **Online Courses and Learning Platforms:**

   - **Coursera:** Offers a range of courses on topics such as business growth, entrepreneurship, and strategic management. Check out courses like "Scaling Operations: Linking Strategy and Execution" or "Entrepreneurship 101: Who is Your Customer?"

   - **Udemy:** Provides a wide variety of courses on scaling businesses, leadership, and strategic planning. Consider courses like "Business Strategy: Build a Successful Business Model" or "Scaling Your Startup: People, Processes, and Systems."

   - **LinkedIn Learning:** Offers courses and video tutorials on various aspects of business growth, leadership development, and organizational management. Explore courses like *"Strategic Planning Foundations"* or *"Leading and Working in Teams."*

3. **Business Blogs and Websites:**

- **Harvard Business Review (HBR):** HBR publishes insightful articles and case studies on business strategy, leadership, and innovation. Visit their website to access a wealth of resources.

- **Entrepreneur:** A leading publication that covers various aspects of entrepreneurship, growth strategies, and emerging trends in business. Their website provides articles, expert advice, and success stories.

- **Inc.:** Inc. is a resourceful platform that offers practical tips, thought leadership, and success stories for growing businesses. Explore their articles and resources on scaling and sustaining business growth.

4. **Industry-specific Publications:**

   - Industry associations, trade magazines, and professional publications in your specific field can provide valuable insights and best practices tailored to your industry. Stay updated with the latest trends, research, and case studies relevant to your sector.

5. **Podcasts:**

   - *"The Scaling Up Business Podcast"* hosted by Verne Harnish: Provides practical insights and interviews with successful entrepreneurs and business leaders on scaling and growing businesses.

   - *"The Tim Ferriss Show":* Tim Ferriss interviews top performers from various fields, uncovering their strategies, habits, and experiences that contribute to their success.

Remember to approach these resources with a curious mindset, seeking knowledge and inspiration to fuel your growth journey. Continuously explore, learn, and adapt the insights to your specific business context. These resources will serve as valuable references and inspire you to explore new strategies and approaches as you scale and sustain your business expansion.

Stay committed to your growth goals and never stop learning. The journey of business expansion is an ongoing process, and these resources will help you navigate the challenges and embrace the opportunities that lie ahead.

Section 2: Professional Organizations, Networking Groups, and Conferences

Engaging with professional organizations, networking groups, and conferences can provide entrepreneurs with valuable opportunities to expand their network, gain industry-specific knowledge, and stay updated with the latest trends. Here are some relevant resources to consider:

1. **Professional Organizations:**

   - **Chamber of Commerce:** Local and regional chambers of commerce offer networking events, business development resources, and advocacy for small businesses. Joining your local chamber can help you connect with other entrepreneurs and access valuable resources.

   - **Industry-Specific Associations:** Explore industry-specific associations and organizations related to your business sector. These associations often host conferences, webinars, and networking events tailored to the industry's needs.

2. **Networking Groups:**

- **Meetup:** Meetup is a platform that connects people with similar interests and facilitates networking events and meetings. Look for relevant business or industry-specific Meetup groups in your area to connect with like-minded entrepreneurs.

- **LinkedIn Groups:** Join LinkedIn groups that align with your industry or business interests. Engage in discussions, ask questions, and connect with professionals in your field.

3. **Conferences and Events:**

- **Industry Conferences:** Attend conferences and industry events related to your sector. These gatherings offer opportunities to learn from industry experts, gain insights into emerging trends, and network with key players in your field.

- **Entrepreneurship Conferences:** Explore entrepreneurship-focused conferences, such as Startup Grind, TechCrunch Disrupt, or the Global Entrepreneurship Summit. These events bring together entrepreneurs, investors, and thought leaders from various industries.

Section 3: Government Programs, Grants, and Funding Opportunities

Government programs, grants, and funding opportunities can provide vital support for business growth and development. Here are a few avenues to explore:

1. **Small Business Administration (SBA):** The SBA offers resources, training programs, and access to loans and grants for small businesses. Their website provides information on various funding options, including the Small Business Innovation Research (SBIR) program and the Small Business Investment Company (SBIC) program.

2. **Economic Development Agencies:** Local and regional economic development agencies often provide support, grants, and incentives for businesses looking to expand or relocate. Research the agencies in your area and inquire about available programs.

3. **Venture Capital and Angel Investor Networks:** Consider seeking investment from venture capital firms or connecting with angel investor networks. These entities provide funding and mentorship for startups and high-growth businesses.

Section 4: Brief Descriptions and Reviews of Resources

1. **Professional Organizations, Networking Groups, and Conferences:** These resources offer opportunities to connect with industry peers, gain insights from experts, and stay updated with industry trends. By participating in events and engaging with like-minded professionals,

you can expand your network and access valuable knowledge-sharing platforms.

2. **Government Programs, Grants, and Funding Opportunities:** Government support programs, grants, and funding opportunities can provide financial assistance, mentorship, and access to resources that can fuel your business growth. These initiatives aim to foster entrepreneurship, innovation, and economic development.

By leveraging these resources, you can tap into a broader network, gain industry-specific knowledge, and access financial support. Remember to research each resource thoroughly, assess its relevance to your business goals, and actively engage with the opportunities they offer. Networking and accessing funding programs can significantly contribute to your business growth and development, allowing you to navigate challenges and seize new opportunities in your industry.

SWOT Analysis Worksheet

Strengths	Weaknesses
Identify the unique qualities, resources, or capabilities that give your business a competitive advantage.	Identify the areas where your business may be lacking or could improve.
Consider your internal strengths, such as a strong brand reputation, skilled employees, or proprietary technology.	Assess internal factors that may hinder your growth or limit your competitiveness, such as limited financial resources or outdated infrastructure.
List your strengths in the designated section of the worksheet.	List your weaknesses in the designated section of the worksheet.
Opportunities	**Threats**
Identify external factors or trends that present opportunities for your business.	Identify external factors or challenges that could pose a threat to your business.
Consider market trends, emerging technologies, changes in consumer behavior, or untapped market segments.	Assess competitive pressures, regulatory changes, economic downturns, or disruptive technologies.

Opportunities	Threats
List the opportunities you have identified in the designated section of the worksheet.	List the threats you have identified in the designated section of the worksheet.

Once you have completed the worksheet, analyze the relationships between the different elements of your SWOT analysis:

- **Strengths vs. Opportunities:** Identify how you can leverage your strengths to capitalize on the opportunities available to your business.

- **Strengths vs. Threats:** Determine how your strengths can help mitigate or overcome the threats facing your business.

- **Weaknesses vs. Opportunities:** Explore strategies to address your weaknesses and take advantage of the opportunities in your industry.

- **Weaknesses vs. Threats:** Develop plans to minimize the impact of your weaknesses and protect your business from potential threats.

Remember, a SWOT analysis is an iterative process that requires continuous evaluation and adjustment. Use this table as a starting point to gain insights into your business's current state and identify areas for improvement. By leveraging your strengths, addressing weaknesses, capitalizing on opportunities, and managing threats, you can develop strategies to drive sustainable growth and maintain a competitive edge in your industry.

Cultural Fit Assessment Worksheet

Core Values	Candidate Alignment
Beliefs	Rating (e.g., high, medium; or low, 1 – 5). Specific comments.
Ethics	Rating (e.g., high, medium; or low, 1 – 5). Specific comments.
Attitudes towards Work	Rating (e.g., high, medium; or low, 1 – 5). Specific comments.
Company Culture	**Candidate Fit**
Communication Style	Rating (e.g., high, medium; or low, 1 – 5). Specific comments.
Work Environment Preferences	Rating (e.g., high, medium; or low, 1 – 5). Specific comments.
Collaboration	Rating (e.g., high, medium; or low, 1 – 5). Specific comments.
Team Dynamics	**Candidate Compatibility**
Ability to Work Collaboratively	Rating (e.g., high, medium; or low, 1 – 5). Specific comments.
Adaptability	Rating (e.g., high, medium; or low, 1 – 5). Specific comments.
Interpersonal Skills	Rating (e.g., high, medium; or low, 1 – 5). Specific comments.

Once you have completed the worksheet, assess the candidate's cultural fit based on the following considerations:

1. **Core Values**: Evaluate how well the candidate's values align with the core values of your company. Consider their beliefs, ethics, and attitudes towards work.

2. **Company Culture:** Assess how the candidate would fit within your company's culture. Consider aspects such as communication style, work environment preferences, and collaboration.

3. **Team Dynamics:** Determine if the candidate's personality and working style would complement the existing team members. Consider their ability to work collaboratively, adaptability, and interpersonal skills.

For each section, indicate the level of alignment or compatibility on a scale (e.g., high, medium, low) or provide specific comments. You may also define a numerical rating system.

Remember, cultural fit is an essential aspect of building a cohesive and harmonious team. By evaluating candidates based on their alignment with your core values, company culture, and team dynamics, you can make more informed hiring decisions and increase the likelihood of long-term success and satisfaction for both the candidate and your organization.

Thank you.